HEIDEGGER:
A GUIDE FOR THE PERPLEXED

Continuum *Guides for the Perplexed*

Continuum's Guides for the Perplexed are clear, concise and accessible introductions to thinkers, writers and subjects that students and readers can find especially challenging. Concentrating specifically on what it is that makes the subject difficult to grasp, these books explain and explore key themes and ideas, guiding the reader towards a thorough understanding of demanding material.

Guides for the Perplexed available from Continuum:

Adorno: A Guide for the Perplexed, Alex Thomson
Deleuze: A Guide for the Perplexed, Claire Colebrook
Derrida: A Guide for the Perplexed, Julian Wolfreys
Descartes: A Guide for the Perplexed, Justin Skirry
Existentialism: A Guide for the Perplexed, Stephen Earnshaw
Freud: A Guide for the Perplexed, Céline Surprenant
Gadamer: A Guide for the Perplexed, Chris Lawn
Habermas: A Guide for the Perplexed, Eduardo Mendieta
Hegel: A Guide for the Perplexed, David James
Hobbes: A Guide for the Perplexed, Stephen J. Finn
Hume: A Guide for the Perplexed, Angela Coventry
Husserl: A Guide for the Perplexed, Matheson Russell
Kant: A Guide for the Perplexed, T. K. Seung
Kierkegaard: A Guide for the Perplexed, Clare Carlisle
Leibniz: A Guide for the Perplexed, Franklin Perkins
Levinas: A Guide for the Perplexed, B. C. Hutchens
Merleau-Ponty: A Guide for the Perplexed, Eric Matthews
Nietzsche: A Guide for the Perplexed, R. Kevin Hill
Plato: A Guide for the Perplexed, Gerald A. Press
Quine: A Guide for the Perplexed, Gary Kemp
Ricoeur: A Guide for the Perplexed, David Pellauer
Rousseau: A Guide for the Perplexed, Matthew Simpson
Sartre: A Guide for the Perplexed, Gary Cox
Spinoza: A Guide for the Perplexed, Charles Jarrett
Wittgenstein: A Guide for the Perplexed, Mark Addis

HEIDEGGER: A GUIDE FOR THE PERPLEXED

DAVID R. CERBONE

continuum

Continuum International Publishing Group
The Tower Building   80 Maiden Lane
11 York Road   Suite 704
London SE1 7NX   New York NY 10038

www.continuumbooks.com

Excerpts throughout totalling 800 words from POETRY, LANGUAGE,
THOUGHT by MARTIN HEIDEGGER
Translations and Introduction by Albert Hofstadter. Copyright © 1971 by
Martin Heidegger.
Reprinted by permission of HarperCollins Publishers

Excerpts throughout totalling 745 words from THE QUESTION
CONCERNING TECHNOLOGY AND OTHER ESSAYS by
MARTIN HEIDEGGER
Translated and with an Introduction by William Lovitt. English language
translation copyright © 1977 by Harper & Row, Publishers, Inc.
Reprinted by permission of HarperCollins Publishers

Excerpts throughout totalling 350 words from WHAT IS CALLED
THINKING? by MARTIN HEIDEGGER
Translated by Fred D. Wieck and J. Glenn Gray. English translation copyright
© 1968 by Harper & Row, Publishers, Inc.
Reprinted by permission of HarperCollins Publishers

Reprinted by permission from *Being and Time: A Translation of* Sein und Zeit
by Martin Heidegger, translated by Joan Stambaugh, the State University of
New York Press © 1996, State University of New York. All rights reserved.

British Library Cataloguing-in-Publication Data
A catalogue record for this book is available from the British Library.

ISBN-10: HB: 0-8264-8668-1
PB: 0-8264-8669-X
ISBN-13: HB: 978-0-8264-8668-4
PB: 978-0-8264-8669-1

Library of Congress Cataloging-in-Publication Data
A catalog record for this book is available from the Library of Congress.

Typeset by Servis Filmsetting Ltd, Manchester
Printed and bound in Great Britain by MPG Books Ltd, Bodmin, Cornwall

CONTENTS

ACKNOWLEDGMENTS

In order to be a more manageable guide, I have refrained from citing much in the way of the voluminous secondary work on Heidegger's philosophy. This is not to say that I have not over the years profited greatly from the availability of such work, as well as from my many conversations with those who produced what I consider to be the best of it. I would especially like to thank Hubert Dreyfus, with whom I first studied *Being and Time* and from whom I continue to learn. Bert's impact on my thinking about Heidegger is immeasurable and his influence is apparent on every page of this book, even at those places where my reading of Heidegger departs considerably from his (the departures would not be what they are except as responses to his interpretations). Many others have affected my understanding of Heidegger, instructing me on points where I felt perplexed and stimulating me to think things out on my own. Many thanks to William Blattner, William Bracken, Taylor Carman, Steven Crowell, Charles Guignon, John Haugeland, Randall Havas, Stephan Käufer, Sean Kelly, Cristina Lafont, Jeff Malpas, Wayne Martin, Edward Minar, Mark Okrent, Joseph Rouse, Ted Schatzki, Joseph Schear, Hans Sluga and Mark Wrathall.

I would also like to thank the many students over the last several years, on whom I have tried out various ways of making Heidegger intelligible. I know that I have profited greatly from these experiments (and I hope that some of them at least would say the same). Thanks as well to Sarah Campbell and Tom Crick at Continuum for their patience and assistance.

ACKNOWLEDGMENTS

Finally, I would like to acknowledge the love and support of my parents, Anne and Ralph, and especially my wife, Lena, my two boys, Henry and Lowell, and my little girl, Margot, who arrived in the midst of writing this book.

ABBREVIATIONS

The following texts are cited parenthetically in the text by means of abbreviations. Translations have been modified slightly in some cases.

BP   *The Basic Problems of Phenomenology*, trans. A. Hofstadter, Bloomington: Indiana University Press (revised edn), 1982.

BT   *Being and Time*, trans. J. Stambaugh, Albany: State University of New York Press, 1996.

In addition to the Stambaugh translation, there is a long-standing and widely used translation by John Macquarrie and Edward Robinson (New York: Harper and Row, 1962). To facilitate reference to the Macquarrie and Robinson transla-tion, as well as the original German text, I will cite passages from *Being and Time* using both the page number of the Stambaugh translation and the page number of the German text, which appears in the margins of both English transla-tions. The first page number will be for the Stambaugh edition; the second will be the marginal German page number.

DT   *Discourse on Thinking*, trans. J. M. Anderson and E. H. Freund, New York: Harper and Row, 1966.

HCT   *The History of the Concept of Time: Prologomena*, trans. T. Kisiel, Bloomington: Indiana University Press, 1985.

OBT   *Off the Beaten Track*, ed. and trans. J. Young and K. Haynes, Cambridge: Cambridge University Press, 2002.

OWL   *On the Way to Language*, trans. P. D. Hertz, New York: Harper and Row, 1971.

PLT   *Poetry, Language, Thought*, trans. A. Hofstadter, New York: Harper and Row, 1971.

QCT   *The Question Concerning Technology and Other Essays*, trans. W. Lovitt, New York: Harper and Row, 1977.

WCT *What Is Called Thinking?*, trans. J. G. Gray, New York: Harper and Row, 1968.

Further information about Heidegger's writings and their availability in English can be found at the end of the book.

The passages from Arthur Eddington's *The Nature of the Physical World* are taken from the excerpt, 'Two Tables' in *Reality*, ed. C. Levenson and J. Westphal, Indianapolis: Hackett Publishing, 1994, pp. 144–9.

INTRODUCTION

Anyone contemplating reading this book has, I will assume, at least contemplated, and perhaps even tried, reading some of Heidegger's philosophy, and has, I will further assume, found doing so, or even the prospect of doing so, anything ranging from daunting to intimidating to off-putting to downright bewildering. Heidegger's writing is no doubt challenging, indeed the term used in the title to this book, 'perplexed', would appear to be particularly apt for describing the state of most newcomers to his work. However, I want to suggest that the term is particularly apt for a rather different reason, since *perplexity* is in many ways precisely the state that Heidegger wants to cultivate in his readers, which implies that his readers, especially newcomers to his work, do not initially or automatically partake of such a state. That is, Heidegger's worry, his worry specifically about our readiness for philosophy, is that we are not sufficiently perplexed, that we instead find ourselves, variously, complacent, inattentive, forgetful or unreflective. Consider, for example, Heidegger's rather astonishing claim in one place that in order to 'learn thinking', we must first admit 'that we are not yet capable of thinking' (WCT, p. 3). Such a remark is intended to be, literally, thought-provoking, and its underlying message is that we are not provoked to think often enough, indeed that we are not yet even in a position to recognize anything that we do as actually thinking. The 'task of thinking', as Heidegger sometimes refers to his philosophy later in his life, requires first a disruption of our complacency, a willingness to acknowledge that we may not yet know what thinking is, and so a willingness to encourage and sustain in ourselves a feeling of perplexity. To dismiss or disown such feelings, to remove them hastily or artificially by means of some form of distraction (superficial entertainment, amusement, intoxication and so on), is to refuse to begin the hard work of thinking philosophically, indeed of really thinking at all. For Heidegger, then, a feeling of perplexity is anything but a reason to put his writings aside; instead, it is precisely what the reader should have if she is to find anything worthwhile in his philosophy.

Heidegger's remarks about thinking come from work written well on in his philosophical career, from a phase commonly referred to as 'the later Heidegger' (the nature and significance of these demarcations will occupy us shortly). The idea, though, that philosophy begins with perplexity can be found throughout his writings. His landmark work written much earlier in his career, *Being and Time*, which we will spend the majority of this book examining, begins with an epigraph taken from Plato's dialogue, *Sophist*:

> For manifestly you have long been aware of what you mean when you use the expression *'being'*. We, however, who used to think we understood it, have now become perplexed.

Heidegger no doubt intends this admission of perplexity to describe his own condition, but his hope is that the 'we' who speak here will come to include his readership as well. His fear is that it may not. Heidegger follows this citation with the question of whether we currently have an answer to the question of the meaning of the word 'being', and his answer is emphatically negative. He then raises a further question concerning our attitude toward our lack of an answer to the question of being: he asks after the perplexity we may or may not feel about our current predicament with respect to the notion of being: 'But are we nowadays even perplexed at our inability to understand the expression "being"', to which Heidegger replies, 'Not at all' (BT, p. xix/1). Heidegger thus sees as his principal challenge in *Being and Time* to be one of bringing his readers to the point of feeling perplexed, of finding the 'question of being' an occasion for puzzlement. Without that perplexity, without being struck both by the question of being and our inability to answer it immediately, Heidegger's investigation cannot even begin to make sense, much less appear compelling, even vital. So again, I want to suggest that perplexity in the face of Heidegger's philosophy is a good thing, something to be cultivated and investigated, and so a reader who finds herself perplexed should be praised as long as she is willing to see in that perplexity a reason to continue rather than simply put Heidegger's writings aside.

As a 'guide for the perplexed', the task of this book is perhaps to alleviate some of that perplexity, though it would be inadvisable to try to remove it altogether. Instead, my aim is to effect a kind of reorientation with respect to that perplexity, so that it may be engaged with productively. Meeting this aim will require distinguishing carefully between perplexity, a healthy and potentially fruitful state, from mere *confusion*, a more scattered, dissonant condition that serves only to stifle investigation. Heidegger's writings are indeed perplexing – as I've already tried to suggest, they aim to be perplexing – but they can be confusing as well, and I see my job as one of diminishing that confusion so that we may feel perplexed in the right way. I thus do *not* see my job as one of simply making Heidegger 'easy' or 'simple', since attempting to do so could only distort what Heidegger is up to in his philosophy (I actually think this is the case for trying to understand any serious philosopher – Kant, Plato, Hegel or Aristotle can no more be made easy without falsification than Heidegger). Making Heidegger easy would short-circuit the perplexity that Heidegger himself regards as necessary for his philosophy to be properly understood and appreciated; simplification would provide the appearance of comprehension, along with the even more harmful conclusion that any further thought could be foregone. I want instead, by removing confusion, to provide a kind of foothold for engaging with Heidegger's writings, so that the reader may learn from them, question them, quarrel with them and perhaps even extend the kind of thinking they initiate. All of these things can only be properly done insofar as one is not just confused about what Heidegger is saying. I have found over the years of teaching Heidegger that my more confused students are especially apt to be quarrelsome, though this typically amounts to little more than lashing out, rather than anything approaching illuminating debate. Any series of angry observations that can be condensed into the lament, 'Heidegger sucks!' is far indeed from the kind of *thinking* Heidegger's philosophy wishes to enact and encourage in its audience. In my view, Heidegger's philosophy does not 'suck', indeed quite the contrary. There is much to be learned from engaging seriously and patiently with his writings, and my hope is that this book will help readers in doing so.

Heidegger's writings are expansive and by no means monolithic in their philosophical outlook. Heidegger lived and worked for a very long time and his views changed considerably over the years. The most significant 'break' in his thinking is between the period in which he wrote *Being and Time* – what is often referred to as Heidegger's 'early philosophy' – and pretty much everything thereafter. (Scholars do on occasion distinguish between a 'middle' and a later Heidegger, and lately there has been a call by some to recognize an 'earliest' Heidegger as well. While there is considerable merit in these finer-grained distinctions, the coarser division will suffice for our purposes.) Despite the fact that the later philosophy occupies by far the majority of Heidegger's philosophical career (more than four decades versus roughly one), the majority of this book will be devoted to *Being and Time*. Though Heidegger's philosophy changes considerably, sometimes in ways that explicitly repudiate claims and methods central to *Being and Time*, he never entirely abandons that early work and it continues to serve as a kind of touchstone for all of his thinking. Thus, in order to understand any of Heidegger's work, it is necessary to have a good grip on what he is up to in *Being and Time*. Of course, getting a good grip on *Being and Time* is important not just as a means to understanding the later philosophy. There is a great deal of tremendous philosophical importance in *Being and Time*, well worth considering for its own sake and for its impact on philosophy well beyond his own later writings. As I'll try to demonstrate at various places below, Heidegger's insights and ideas in *Being and Time* have an impact on some of the very basic ways in which we think about our relation to the world, as many of those ways have been informed by philosophical ideas that he exposes as deeply problematic. *Being and Time* is not only an exercise in philosophical criticism, however, as it offers a rich and compelling conception of human existence that proved deeply influential for the development of the existentialist tradition culminating in Jean-Paul Sartre's philosophy of the 1940s (Heidegger, for his part, was not entirely pleased that his earlier work had this effect). Throughout Part I, we will work through *Being and Time* with an eye toward both its critical and productive aspects.

Part II will be devoted to Heidegger's later philosophy. Owing to the extent of his later work, my coverage here will be even more selective than with *Being and Time*. I will try, though, to present several of what I take to be key ideas in the later work and situate them in relation to his earlier work. Though I have left a great deal out, my hope is that by reading this book, the perplexed, rather than confused, reader will be well equipped to work through what's been omitted on his or her own.

PART I

HEIDEGGER'S EARLY PHILOSOPHY

CHAPTER 1

THE QUESTION OF BEING AND
BEING AND TIME

In my introductory remarks, I appealed to the epigraph of *Being and Time*, taken from Plato's *Sophist*, as illustrative of the kind of perplexity Heidegger wishes to awaken and cultivate in his readership. More specifically, the perplexity Heidegger invites concerns what he calls simply 'the question of being' (or *Seinsfrage*), which is meant to serve as the subject matter of the entirety of *Being and Time* (and beyond, as I'll explain below). Heidegger's opening remarks are meant to suggest that Western philosophy has slowly but surely whittled away at the perplexity felt by the ancient Greeks, with whom the question of being, Heidegger claims, first arose. The kind of wonder or astonishment felt by the Greeks in the presence of reality, and so their wonder and astonishment at the question of what it means to be, has slowly and lamentably faded as Western philosophy has developed: the question of being 'sustained the avid research of Plato and Aristotle but then on ceased to be heard *as a thematic question of actual investigation*' (BT, p. 1/2). Too often, the question of being has simply been ignored, or, worse, taken to admit all too easily of an answer. A facile answer, Heidegger thinks, is tantamount to ignoring the question, i.e. the question is answered in a way that really amounts to little more than a quick dismissal. Heidegger canvasses three of these ready answers to the question of being in the opening paragraphs of his first Introduction – being is the 'most universal' concept; being is 'indefinable'; and being is 'self-evident' – none of which Heidegger finds satisfactory, and all of which point only to the need for further investigation. (That being is universal does not mean that its meaning is clear; that being is indefinable does not eliminate the question of its meaning; and that the meaning is self-evident and yet we find ourselves at a loss to say what it means

3

only shows that we are more in the dark than we care to admit.) Thus, part of the burden of Heidegger's first Introduction is to impress upon us that the question of being is *the* most fundamental philosophical question, though the obscurity of the question, due in part to centuries of philosophical distortion and neglect, means that formulating the question properly and setting out to answer the question will require considerable care.

1A DA-SEIN AND THE QUESTION OF BEING

After his opening remarks concerning the need to revisit the question of being and reconsider its formulation, Heidegger devotes the majority of the first Introduction to devising and justifying a strategy for clarifying and answering the question of being. The strategy focuses on the nature of human existence, which Heidegger refers to using the term 'Da-sein'. The term is left untranslated in English editions of *Being and Time*, largely to signal the peculiarity of Heidegger's terminology even in German. The term '*Dasein*' is not one coined by Heidegger: my nearest German dictionary lists '*dasein*' as a verb meaning 'to exist' or 'to be there', and also '*Dasein*' as a noun meaning 'presence', 'existence' and 'life'. To disrupt any assimilation of Heidegger's usage to these standard meanings, the Stambaugh translation inserts a hyphen between the two component terms ('*da*', meaning 'here' or 'there', and '*sein*', meaning 'being'); in her own introduction, she explains the addition of the hyphen as conforming to Heidegger's own directives (see *BT*, p. xiv). Heidegger's appropriation of the term for one kind of being or entity is thus idiosyncratic, and deliberately so: Heidegger wants to reserve a special term for the kind of beings we are that does not carry with it any unwanted connotations or prejudices, as is often the case if we use locutions such as 'human being', '*homo sapiens*', 'man' and so on. These terms are beset by various, potentially misleading, anthropological, biological and even theological ideas that will only serve to distract. For example, Heidegger does not want his conclusions regarding what is fundamental and distinctive about our way of being to be circumscribed by the facts of biology: it is perfectly conceivable on Heidegger's account that biologically different beings, even wildly different ones (suppose, for example, that we some day encounter extraterrestrials), exhibit these same characteristics or features. Thus, '*homo sapiens*' as principally a biological categorization is incorrect for Heidegger's purposes. What is distinctive about Da-sein, as the entity each of us is, is not a matter of biology or theology, but rather characteristics that are to be exhibited and worked out *phenomenologically* (just what that means will be spelled out later on).

Consider again the perplexity that we feel (or, from Heidegger's perspective, we *ought* to feel) upon first hearing the question of being. Insofar as we understand the question at all, i.e. insofar as we respond with something more than 'Huh?' or 'Say what?' it is still likely to be the case that we will very quickly run out of things to say. Certain other terms may spring to mind or to our lips – reality, actuality, existence and so on – but spelling out what *these* terms really mean appears to be no less daunting than our trying to say what 'being' means. Heidegger fully expects this kind of difficulty; all he asks initially is that we not forego the difficulty and that we not interpret our difficulty as a basis for condemning the question. By way of reassurance, perhaps, he is quick to point out that we are not as lacking in resources as we might feel. In fact, *we* turn out to be the principal 'resource' for answering the question of being, though that piece of information may no doubt come as a surprise.

To see what Heidegger has in mind here, let us consider two perplexing claims he enters in the first Introduction:

1. Da-sein is a being whose being is an issue for it.
2. Da-sein is a being who has an understanding of being.

Claim (2) for Heidegger holds the key to making progress in clarifying and answering the question of being: that Da-sein is a being who has an understanding of being means that Da-sein is a good place to look to get started. In other words, since Da-sein already understands what Heidegger wants to know the meaning of (namely, being), then Da-sein is the best clue available for working out what it means for anything to be. While this is roughly Heidegger's reasoning, it is still rather schematic: we need to know more about just what (1) and (2) mean, how they are interconnected and how Heidegger plans to exploit them to further his philosophical project.

On the face of it, (1) and (2) just sound like two different ideas, both of which may happen to be true about us (or about Da-sein). For Heidegger, however, (1) and (2) are importantly interconnected. A general lesson about reading *Being and Time* is in the offing here: rarely for Heidegger is a series of claims he enters on a particular topic merely a number of things that happen to be true about the topic; they are nearly always connected by relations of derivation, implication and interdependence. This is evident in Heidegger's frequent talk of something's being a 'unitary phenomenon' and of two notions being 'equiprimordial' or equally fundamental. The interconnectedness of (1) and (2) is just one example, but an important one. Indeed, I would contend that the relation Heidegger claims (1) stands in to (2) is one of the most important ideas in *Being and Time*.

To begin working out these ideas and exploring the connections among them, let us first consider the following paragraph from *Being and Time* where they both make their appearance:

> Da-sein is an entity that does not simply occur among other beings. Rather it is ontically distinguished by the fact that in its being this being is concerned *about* its very being. Thus it is constitutive of the being of Da-sein to have, in its very being, a relation of being to this being. And this in turn means that Da-sein understands itself in its being in some way and with some explicitness. It is proper to this being that it be disclosed to itself with and through its being. *Understanding of being is itself a determination of being of Da-sein.* The ontic distinction of Da-sein lies in the fact that it *is* ontological. (BT, p. 10/12)

There is quite a bit going on in this paragraph and unpacking it completely will take some doing. (Notice in particular how Heidegger begins with claim (1) and by the end of the paragraph has reached claim (2), which indicates their interconnected character.) First, though, a bit of terminological clarification concerning the distinction between *ontical* and *ontological* is needed. The distinction is one between entities and their way of being. To consider an entity *ontically* means to consider its particular characteristics as a particular entity or particular kind of entity, whereas to consider that entity *ontologically* means to consider that entity's way of being. Thus, an ontological characterization is one that spells out what it means to *be* that kind of entity, while an ontical characterization enumerates the entity's particular features. Another way to consider the distinction is to think of the ontical as the instantiation of some ontological category or determination. So, for example, the claim that Da-sein is a being whose being is an issue is an *ontological* claim, but the particular way its being is an issue for any particular Da-sein is an *ontical* matter. For Heidegger, disciplines that study human beings such as sociology and anthropology (as well as biology) are all ontical or ontic, since they all investigate particular ways human beings behave and interact, as well as how their internal workings function. All of these disciplines are *positive*, concerned with positive matters of facts, as well as the laws and principles that can be formulated on their basis. Heidegger thinks that the natural sciences are ontical in another respect, in that the sciences by and large work *within* some taken-for-granted understanding of what it is to be the kind of entity studied by the various sciences. When, however, a science suffers a crisis, such that the question of what that taken-for-granted domain really comes to, then it begins to approach ontological inquiry. If a physicist steps back and asks, 'Just what is meant by "physical" anyway?' or, 'How do we demarcate the domain of the physical?', then she is raising ontological, rather than ontical, questions.

To return to the paragraph, Heidegger is here claiming, first, that Da-sein is 'ontically distinguished' from other entities by the fact that it does not 'just occur' among them. Da-sein, of course, does occur among other entities: as I work at my desk writing this, I stand in various spatial relations, for example, to my desk and the various items on it, as well as the floor, the door to my study and the hallway outside it (indeed, I stand in *some* spatial relation to any and every entity in the universe). Da-sein is thus a being among or alongside other entities, but there is something further to be said by way of characterizing Da-sein that marks it out as an altogether different kind of being than all the other entities that occur. What is distinctive is registered in the second sentence of the paragraph, which is precisely claim (1): Da-sein is distinctive in that its being is an *issue* for it. But what does this mean? The basic idea is this: to say that Da-sein's being is an issue for it is to say that Da-sein is a being that can and does confront its own existence, and that it confronts its own existence as something to be worked out or determined. That is, Da-sein's own existence is present to it as a matter of ongoing concern: the idea that its being is an issue for it includes both these ideas, its being present and being a matter of concern. Confrontations of this sort happen explicitly from time to time – when we ask ourselves what we really want to be, or worry about who we really are, or wonder about the point of something we're doing, or try to decide if some project we've embarked upon is what we really want to be

7

doing and so on – but Heidegger's claim is meant to be more general: our being is *always* an issue, since we are always in the process of working out what it is to be the beings that we are, even when we do not stop to think explicitly about it. That our existence is always an issue is indicated by the fact that we *can* always stop and reflect explicitly on where our lives are going and on how we want our lives to look, but even if we do not stop to reflect, our lives are going one way or another and taking shape so as to have a particular look to them. As such, our existence is a matter of concern for us, even when that concern amounts to nearly complete disregard (indifference towards one's own existence is something Heidegger would regard as a 'deficient' mode of concern).

That we can take up such attitudes as indifference and concern towards our own existence signals our uniqueness in comparison with other kinds of entities. Other kinds of entities 'just occur'. We can see this most readily if we consider inanimate objects, such as a rock I find lying in a field or the desk in my study: what it is to be a rock or a desk is not something that is of concern or at issue *for* the rock or *for* the desk. (I might worry about where I found the rock, whether throwing it is a good idea and so on, but none of that is something the rock has any stake in; likewise, I may worry that my desk has become too messy, that it might look better elsewhere in my study, that I'd be happier with something more sleek and modern and so on, but again, none of this is of concern *to* the desk.) Neither of these entities confronts its own existence in any way, nor is there anything either of them does by way of working out or determining their respective ways of being. Heidegger would also claim, more controversially perhaps, that even other *animate* objects, i.e. animals, do not confront their own existence as an issue. For Heidegger, an animal is, one might say, 'hard-wired' to act out a predetermined set of instinctual drives in response to the particulars of the environment that the animal finds itself in. Nothing about those drives is an issue for the animal, which means, among other things, that there are no attitudes the animal can adopt towards the drives it happens to have. (This is not to deny that animals 'try' to stay alive, but such striving for survival is just one more hard-wired disposition or instinct, and so is not something the animal in any way chooses, reflects upon or can change.) For any such non-Da-sein entity, its 'being is a matter of "indifference," more precisely, it "is" in such a way that its being can neither be indifferent nor non-indifferent to it' (BT, p. 40/42). Heidegger adds the more precise formulation to make it clear that the range of attitudes characteristic of Da-sein pertains only to Da-sein: my desk neither cares nor does not care about its existence; the same is true for the deer I see occasionally outside my study window. That these attitudes pertain exclusively to Da-sein means that no other entity bears this kind of relation to its own existence, i.e. other kinds of entities do not confront their own existence as a matter of concern, as something to be determined or worked out.

1B DA-SEIN AND THE UNDERSTANDING OF BEING

Da-sein is thus distinctive in that the question of what it is to be Da-sein is one that it can and does confront. To say that Da-sein 'is onto-logical', which means that the capacity to raise and work out the question of being, in particular its own being, is part and parcel of what it is to be Da-sein. Da-sein is a being that confronts the question of what it is to be that being, and, by extension, the question of what it means to be anything at all. If we reflect further on this 'capacity', we will find ourselves very quickly in the vicinity of claim (2), since all of this talk of Da-sein's 'confronting' its existence, of 'raising' and 'working out' the question of what it means to be the being that it is, clearly implies that Da-sein has some *understanding* of the kind of being it is, indeed an understanding of its own way of being *as* something to be worked out or determined; hence Heidegger's emphatic claim that '*understanding of being is itself a determination of being of Da-sein*'. Considerable care is needed in spelling out the idea that Da-sein has an understanding of being, or that it is ontological, since it would be wrong, and quite obviously so, to conclude from this that we all already have an answer to the question of being. If that were the case, then we would have none of the perplexity or confusion we experience upon first hearing the question raised (nor would we have anything to learn from reading *Being and Time*). Shortly after the paragraph we are considering, Heidegger will qualify his claim concerning Da-sein's understanding of being as being *pre-ontological*, which serves to indicate that the understanding of being Da-sein (always) possesses is not usually to any great degree explicit or 'thematic'. Instead, Da-sein's under-standing is largely implicit, manifest primarily in how it acts, rather than what it explicitly thinks. We do not, that is, already have a *theory* of being (as Heidegger says, 'To be ontological does not yet mean to develop ontology' (BT, p. 10/12)), but instead we think, talk and act in ways that register some sensitivity to different ways for entities to be. We can see this in our general facility with respect to various forms of the verb 'to be', i.e. we are all generally competent with respect to what it means to say of something that it *is* (and *was*, and *will be*) and this includes having at least a vague sense that 'is' means something different when spoken of with respect to different kinds of entities. For example, when we say:

1. There is a prime number between four and six

and

2. There is a squirrel in the tree over there

we understand each of these as entering related claims, in that each of them makes a claim regarding the existence and location of something, a prime number in one case, a squirrel in the other, and yet we also feel there to be something quite different going on in each case, for example in the sense that prime numbers are not the kind of thing one might find in a tree and that squirrels are not found between four and six. (Moreover, it makes perfectly clear sense to say that there *was* a squirrel in the tree, whereas it is not immediately clear what it would mean to say that there *was* a prime number between four and six (the existence of numbers would appear to be 'tenseless'). This again suggests a difference in the meaning of 'is' in each case.) We thus have a sense not only that prime numbers and squirrels are different, but that the difference between a prime number and squirrel is a different kind of difference from the difference between a squirrel and, say, a tiger, or even a rock. Now again, this is only something that we have a vague intimation about, which means that we would come up short fairly quickly were we to try to spell out just what these sorts of differences come to.

Though we may come up short when trying to spell out these differences explicitly, we rarely are so confounded when it comes to how we *act*. Consider, for example, the following two commands:

1. Don't come back until you have five dollars for me!
2. Don't come back until you have five good ideas for me!

Each of these commands is relatively straightforward, though perhaps not especially polite, and so we understand straight away what is involved in acting upon them and what would count as fulfilling them. How we act upon each of the requests and how we determine whether the command has been obeyed involves, in each case, markedly different procedures and standards. Ideas and dollars are found and transferred in very different ways. For example, when you've given me your five dollars, you no longer have it, whereas you still have your five ideas when you've also given them to me. The ideas might be conveyed on paper or they might be kept 'in your head' and conveyed via your reporting them to me; the five dollars, by contrast, cannot just be reported, but must instead involve the transfer of a specific quantity of money. Even though few of us have any kind of worked-out theory of what dollars are (we may have some vague ideas about capital, markets and exchange-values, and we may have some further vague sense that money is kind of peculiar in that little metal coins and variously coloured and inscribed pieces of paper are not *intrinsically* worth all that much), nor about ideas (again, we may have a vague sense that ideas are markedly different from things or objects, though when pressed we may go off in all sorts of directions, appealing to special items or processes in the mind or the head, or even the soul, and not all of these directions may be especially fruitful or even promising), we still by and large know our way about in dealing with such things, and this again signals the status of our understanding as pre-ontological in Heidegger's sense.

We can now, I think, begin to see just how intertwined claims (1) and (2) are for Heidegger. The idea that Da-sein is a being whose being is an issue for it underwrites the idea that it has an understanding of being: if Da-sein did not confront its own existence as something to be worked out or determined, then there would not be any way(s) in which it understood both its own being and the being of other kinds of entities. I think it would be a mistake, though, to see (1) and (2) as standing in this one-directional relation of dependence, since we can also say that if Da-sein did not have any understanding of being, especially its own, then there is no way in which its being could be an issue for it. We should thus understand (1) and (2) as reciprocally related: spelling out (1) quickly leads to the invocation of (2) and vice versa.

Da-sein, as a being whose being is an issue for it, is a being who has an understanding of being, even if that understanding is not worked out or explicit. That Da-sein has an understanding of *being* gives us a foothold for answering the question of the meaning of being. That is, Heidegger contends that if our way of being *is* worked out or made explicit, this will move us toward an answer to the question of being in general: 'The explicit and lucid formulation of the question of the meaning of being requires a prior suitable explication of a being (Da-sein) with regard to its being' (BT, p. 6/7). Since Da-sein 'possesses – in a manner constitutive of its understanding of existence – an understanding of the being of all beings unlike itself', it is 'ontologically the primary being to be interrogated' (BT, p. 11/13). The first, and for the most part the only, order of business of *Being and Time* is thus to 'interrogate' Da-sein with respect to its way of being: hence, Division One of the work is titled, 'Preparatory Fundamental Analysis of Da-sein', while Division Two is labelled simply, 'Da-sein and Temporality'. Division Two considers Da-sein in its 'authenticity', rather than its 'everydayness', and then begins the unfinished project of explicating Da-sein's way of being, along with the being of other kinds of entities, in terms of time or temporality. It should be noted that the entirety of *Being and Time* was originally envisioned by Heidegger as only the beginning of a larger work: there was to be a third division beyond the extant two, and these three divisions would make up Part One; Part Two was itself to have consisted of three divisions. Heidegger never completed this project, though one can read many of the lecture courses subsequent to *Being and Time*, as well as his book, *Kant and the Problem of Metaphysics*, published in 1929, as at least partial attempts in the direction of this envisioned opus.

CHAPTER 2

HEIDEGGER AND PHENOMENOLOGY

If the first order of business in *Being and Time* is to 'interrogate', 'explicate' and 'analyse' Da-sein's way of being, how are these notions of 'interrogation', 'explication' and 'analysis' to be understood? What sort of method does Heidegger propose for investigating the way of being of Da-sein, along with the meaning of being more generally? In a word, the answer to these questions is, simply, 'phenomenology', though, not surprisingly, working out just what Heidegger means by this term will take quite a few more words. In the second Introduction to *Being and Time*, Heidegger lays out his conception of phenomenology. He does so primarily by appealing to the etymology of the term, tracing the word back to its Greek origins in the two terms for 'phenomenon' and 'logos'. Heidegger's appeal to the origins of the term 'phenomenology' can be seen as an unspoken, but rather obvious, criticism of Edmund Husserl, whose conception of phenomenology would be the most ready resource for Heidegger to mine. That Heidegger does not discuss Husserl's conception of phenomenology, let alone appropriate it for his project in *Being and Time*, but instead claims to be locating a more 'original' or 'primordial' meaning of the term, shows, however subtly, the extent of his disagreements with Husserl. This does not mean that Heidegger has nothing to say about Husserl's conception of phenomenology. If one looks beyond the confines of *Being and Time*, there is a great deal in the way of lecture material devoted to the topic (*The History of the Concept of Time* lectures loom large here, but there are others as well, such as the recently translated *Introduction to Phenomenological Research*). In this lecture material, Heidegger is often careful to single out and praise many of Husserl's achievements in phenomenology (the original 'breakthrough' to phenomenology in Husserl's *Logical Investigations*, the notion of intentionality and the idea of 'categorial intuition', to name the most prominent), before then proceeding to explain where Husserl went wrong. To get clear, then, about the meaning and significance of Heidegger's conception of phenomenology, it will be helpful to spend a little time on Husserl.

2A THE HUSSERLIAN BACKGROUND

I'm afraid that there is no quick and easy way of saying what Husserl's conception of phenomenology is all about, in part because Husserl himself spent a great deal of effort over several decades rethinking and reformulating just what he took phenomenology to be. However, we need to start somewhere, and it would be best to begin with the notion of *consciousness*: phenomenology, for Husserl, is the study or science of consciousness. This first formulation is still not particularly informative or definitive, since there are all sorts of ways in which one can study, or have a science of, consciousness (consider the ways in which psychology, physiology and neuro-science might all take an interest in consciousness). It might help to say that for Husserl, phenomenology is interested in the notion of consciousness *as* experienced, as opposed, say, to taking an interest in whatever underlying causes consciousness has (in the brain and nervous system, for example), but even this does not distinguish phenomenology from, for example, narrative or 'stream of consciousness' accounts that try to capture the 'feel' of a particular person's experience at a particular time and place. Phenomenology, for Husserl, is not meant to be autobiographical; indeed, it is emphatically not interested in the particular, idiosyncratic features of this or that person's experience at all. Rather, phenomenology as Husserl conceives it is interested in the structure of consciousness in and of itself, regardless of whose consciousness it is *and* regardless of what the underlying causes of consciousness turn out to be.

Another way of putting this is to say that Husserl is trying to determine what the *essence* or *essential structure* of consciousness is, and he thinks that this determination can and must be made independently of questions concerning the underlying causes of consciousness. There are many reasons why Husserl does think this, and canvassing all of them would take us very far afield. For now, it may help simply to consider the following kind of case: imagine we were to encounter a wholly new kind of being, an alien from outer space, for example. Now, it would appear to be conceivable that such a being was conscious, indeed that it enjoyed a great deal in terms of the kinds of experience that we enjoy (visual experience, auditory experience, memory experiences and so on), while at the same time having virtually nothing in common with us physiologically (indeed, we could imagine that this newfound creature was not even a carbon-based life form). If we find this kind of scenario to be imaginable, then we are on the way to accepting some of Husserl's guiding ideas. Insofar as we recognize this imagined being's processes to be consciousness or experience, then there must be structural affinities between those processes and our own, some structures in virtue of which both this being's and our processes *are* experiential processes. At the same time, however, those affinities cannot be ones with respect to underlying causes, since we have imagined the underlying 'machinery' to be wildly different. (This kind of consideration is not decisive, however. Present-day functionalism, for example, would maintain that there could be commonalities in the 'functional role' of our states and those of the being we are imagining, and these commonalities are what underwrite the claim that the being has the same kind of experiences we have. At the same time, none of this bespeaks the presence of the kind of essential structure Husserl has in mind. The intelligibility of the scenario I've described thus only makes us receptive to Husserl's point of view without yet vindicating it.)

Husserl's phenomenology thus enjoins us to focus on our experience solely *as* we experience it, while leaving aside any consideration of what the causes of our experience may be or, indeed, any consideration of whether or not our experience is 'getting it right' with respect to the goings-on in the world. Any beliefs about the sources and success of our experience will only distract from the quest for the essential structure of experience, since, as essential, these structures must obtain regardless of the truth or falsity of any of those beliefs. To avoid these distractions and achieve the kind of focus required, Husserl's phenomenology deploys a very particular strategy, the so-called 'phenomenological reduction', wherein the investigator suspends or 'brackets' all of those beliefs about the sources and success of conscious experience. The investigator thereby 'purifies' his or her experience, which is why Husserl often refers to his brand of phenomenology as *pure* phenomenology.

According to Husserl, the performance of the phenomenological reduction is the necessary first step in the practice of phenomenology. By bracketing or 'putting out of play' all distracting questions and commitments concerning the sources and success of consciousness, the investigator can then describe that 'purified' experience in ways that will reveal its essential structure. This style of investigation is not tantamount to 'introspection', as though phenomenology were trying to find items located 'in' the mind, or more literally in the head for that matter. (If, for example, I pay attention to my current visual experience, that experience is directed entirely outward, to the screen of my computer, the computer housing the screen and the surrounding desk. There is nothing particularly 'inner' about the experience at all.) The principal structures phenomenology seeks concern the *intentionality* of experience, the notion that consciousness is always *of* or *about* something. That is, if we consider what consciousness or experience most fundamentally or essentially is, we find that it always involves the *presentation* and *representation* of things (in the widest sense of the term, since events, states of affairs, abstract ideas and so on can be what a particular episode or stretch of consciousness is of or about). Things are 'given' or 'manifest' in experience, and Husserlian phenomenology seeks to understand the structure of manifestation so as to understand how it is possible at all. (A further claim of Husserlian phenomenology is that by delimiting the essential structure of manifestation, we will thereby gain insight into the essential structure of what is manifest in experience: whatever we can intelligibly think or speak of must be given in experience, and so how something is experienced is a guide to what it can intelligibly be regarded as *being*.)

The essential structures of experience are the structures experience must have in order to have intentionality, in order, that is, to 'give' objects. To get a feel for what Husserl has in mind here, consider a relatively simple example of 'straightforward' perceptual experience, my visual experience of my coffee cup here on my desk. If I reflect carefully on this experience and try to describe it, I might start by noting that the cup is present in my visual field, but not as an isolated entity. I see the cup, but I see it against a background: the cup is seen as sitting on my desk, with the surface of the desk continuing underneath it; a stack of books partially blocks the lower left-hand corner of the cup, and other things (pictures, more books, the wall and so on) are dimly perceived behind it. Insofar as I focus on the cup, the other things mentioned are *only* dimly perceived; otherwise, they could not be a background for my current visual experience of the cup. The idea of figure and ground is an important, even essential element of visual experience. If I concentrate solely on my experience of the cup, I might also notice that while I say that I see the cup, at the same time I only see one side of it, i.e. I see the cup from a particular angle and at a particular distance. Still, the one side that is given in my experience is not flat or isolated: the other sides, though hidden, are nonetheless intimated by my present experience. If I were to reach out and turn the cup, for example, or get up and move to another place in my study, another side of the cup would come into view, while the currently given side of the cup would then be hidden. These experiences of different sides of the cup are predictably organized and arranged: as I turn the cup, the different sides that were until then only intimated come into view in an entirely unsurprising order. Although, as I continue turning, I get different 'looks' or 'views' of the cup, my experience throughout is of *one* cup: I say at each point that I'm seeing *the* cup. This stretch of experience thus has both a kind of unity and plurality to it.

Given even this very brief sketch, we might begin to discern what Husserl would consider structural dimensions of my experience of the cup; moreover, we might also begin to appreciate the claim that these structural dimensions are essential or necessary to my experience being of or about the cup (and other things like it). Consider again the idea of the cup being manifest or given one side at a time: to use Husserl's terminology, the cup is given via 'adumbrations', which again means that I always only see one side of the cup at any given moment of my visual experience. Moreover, Husserl would contend that this is part of what it is to *see* things like cups: such things are, and can only be, given adumbrationally in visual experience. The adumbrational presentations making up my experience of the cup are radically unlike static, free-standing images. They are importantly and dynamically interconnected. Any given adumbration intimates or points to other possible adumbrational presentations of the cup: when I see the cup from the front, the back of the cup is intimated both as hidden and as there to be seen (I do not, for example, experience the back of the cup as coming into existence as I walk around it). Other adumbrational presentations beyond the one currently given in experience are thus part of the *horizon* of that current experience, and when my experience continues so as to reveal those currently intimated, but still hidden sides, they form a *series* with my current adumbrational experience. This formation of a series, so that the various adumbrational presentations are throughout of *one* cup, is what Husserl calls *synthesis*. Again, Husserl would claim that this synthetic-horizonal structure is essential to the possibility of visual experience of material objects like cups. Were we to delete this structure from experience, our experience would never be of or about material objects. If, for example, I were to forget each moment of experience as the next one pops up, or if there were no predictable connection or organization among moments of my experience, then my experience would never add up or amount to being *about* objects. It could perhaps still be a play of images, flashes of momentary sensations, but even here, my experience would be considerably diminished owing to my endemic forgetfulness (indeed, it is not entirely clear to me that we can fully conceive of such radically amnesiac experience). Finally, if we reflect on the essential dimensions of the way material objects are given in visual experience, we can begin to see that we are not just learning about the possibility of experience, but also about material objects: what it is to be a material object is, in part, to be the kind of thing that is given adumbrationally in visual experience (and this visual experience is predictably connected to tactile experience and so on). That, we might say, is part of the meaning of 'material object'.

I want to explore one further detail of Husserl's conception of phenomenology, since it will take us closer to Heidegger's. This aspect of Husserl's phenomenology is one that appears more or less at its inception, in his *Logical Investigations* (the phenomenological reduction, by contrast, did not emerge explicitly in Husserl's thinking until several years later), and is one that considerably impressed Heidegger. If we consider again my visual experience of the cup, how I am inclined to report that experience raises a number of interesting considerations. If I were to report this experience, even to myself, it is unlikely that I would restrict myself to the exclamation, 'Cup!' (there may be occasions where such an exclamation is more likely, for example, if I were to find unexpectedly the coffee cup I had long taken for lost). I may instead say things such as, 'I see the white cup', or, leaving myself out of the report, 'There is my cup'. In working through the example above, we concentrated on the givenness of the cup alone (along with other objects, given as the 'background' to the cup), but this report indicates that there is more than the cup alone that is, or at least can be, given in experience. That is, there are other elements of the report that need to be accounted for beyond just the cup, most notably, 'there is'. My report, and, more importantly, the experience underwriting it, is not merely objectual, the giving of an object in and of itself, but is instead *categorial*: the experience and the report involve a *fact*, the existence of the cup. Categorial experience would appear to require a further explanation or account beyond the simple perception of an object. Take as an example another categorial perception involving my cup underwriting the report, 'The cup is white'. Such a perception involves 'the' and 'is', along with 'cup' and 'white'. Insofar as they are *parts* of my visual experience, they must be so in a way radically different from the cup and its colour. While I straightforwardly see the cup and see the white, saying that I see the cup's *being*-white requires further explanation: *being* is not a part of the cup like its handle, bottom and sides are, nor is it a property of the cup like whiteness and smoothness are. As Kant had famously argued in the *Critique of Pure Reason*, being is not a real property or predicate. Being (along with other categorials) both serve to structure our experience, even of ordinary material objects insofar as they are perceived as playing a role in the apprehension of facts, relations and states of affairs, while at the same time requiring a further phenomenological account beyond the one given for the apprehension of objects alone. In the Sixth Logical Investigation, Husserl argues that while these categorials are not real features of the objects perceived, it would be a mistake to argue that they are some kind of subjective additions to experience, supplied by the mind, say, to complete the sensations afforded by my perceptual organs. Though not 'real' features of the objects we experience, categorials are equally *objective* dimensions of experience (that the cup exists or is white is not a subjective addition to the cup and its colour, but is an objective fact about the world), i.e. they are not subjective, but they are 'given' in a different manner than are objects alone. Indeed, in straightforward perception, the structuring role of categorials is largely unnoticed, though not for that reason unimportant or inessential (without being at least implicitly structured categorially, my perceptual experience could never be such as to license, or even be intelligibly connected to, the assertion, 'I see that the cup is white' or just, 'The cup is white').

For Husserl, the topic of categorial intuition involves two projects: first, explaining the origins in experience of categorial perception or intuition, and then, second, delineating those categorial dimensions more explicitly (so as to account, for example, for the origins of *logic*, which concerns what might be called 'pure' categorials). With regard to the first project, that of accounting for the origins of categorial experience, Husserl's principal claim is that such experiences are *founded* upon the kind of simple apprehension of objects alone. One example he gives is the experience of part–whole relations. If we consider my visual experience of the cup once again, we may imagine it to be rather inactive. I may, that is, during a break from a stretch of writing, simply stop and gaze at my cup without anything in the way of interest or desire. Suppose, however, that I look to the cup during the break and find myself hankering for a cup of coffee. Now, I may look at the cup more attentively and move to inspect it more closely: I may reach out and heft the cup, tipping it slightly so as to look down into its interior. Sadly, I may notice the absence of coffee. I now experience both the cup and the emptiness; indeed, I now experience those two things as *belonging together*, i.e. I have an experience of the form, 'The cup is empty'. I now experience the cup *as* having aspects or properties, which also means that I experience *the* cup as a kind of *whole* or *unity*, precisely as something that has parts or features. Though my categorial experience is founded, again it should be emphasized that it is not merely a subjective mixing or combining of more basic experiences: the categorial apprehension is equally a discernment of something out there in the world, such as the part–whole relations that obtain between the cup and its constituent parts and features.

Documenting phenomenologically the founding relation that obtains between straightforward and categorial intuition is only the beginning of Husserl's account of categorial experience, since those initial categorial experiences can in turn serve to found new kinds of categorial experiences. In these latter experiences, the categorial features of the initially founded experiences are more clearly delineated, so that they become the subject matter of the experiences rather than the ordinary objects experienced. That is, the categorial 'forms' can themselves be the explicit focus of the experience, rather than the 'matter' of the experience: experiences of the form, 'The cup is white' may serve to found experiences of the form, 'S is P', which make explicit a particular meaning of 'is', the 'is' of predication. The 'is' of predication may then be contrasted with the 'is' of identity, and, with sufficient attention, the *laws* obtaining among these categorial forms can be discovered. Husserl, in exploring categorial intuition, is thus concerned to document the phenomenological origins of *logic*, i.e. his aim is to explain the nature and possibility of logically articulated experience. In doing so, he hopes thereby to explain the possibility of *knowledge*, understood as a logically systematic network of judgements. The further details of Husserl's project need not concern us. Our primary concern will be to explore the fate of the notion of categorial intuition in Heidegger's conception of phenomenology and his enactment of it in Division One of *Being and Time*. Such explorations will concern us both momentarily and at later intervals of our examination.

Suffice it to say for now that the idea that *being*, via categorial intuition, can be the subject matter of phenomenology, gives us a clue as to why the young Heidegger was drawn to phenomenology in the first place.

2B PHENOMENON AND LOGOS: HEIDEGGER'S RECONCEPTION

When Heidegger lays out his own conception of phenomenology, it seems far removed from Husserl's methods and concerns. Indeed, he claims that the term 'phenomenology' itself 'does not characterize the "what" of the objects of philosophical research in terms of their content but the "how" of such research' (BT, p. 24/27). Here already we see a departure from Husserl, for whom there is a well-circumscribed domain of inquiry, the phenomena of consciousness (properly understood, of course, so as to avoid any altogether too likely empirical, psychological connotations). Indeed, when Heidegger discusses Husserl explicitly in his lectures, he is especially dismissive of Husserl's preoccupation with consciousness, in particular the idea of consciousness in a purified or 'absolute' sense. Phenomenology, as the 'how' of research, proceeds under the banner, first flown by Husserl, reading 'To the things themselves!' Heidegger explains his understanding of this slogan in the following passage:

The term 'phenomenology' expresses a maxim that can be formulated: 'To the things themselves!' It is opposed to all free-floating constructions and accidental findings; it is also opposed to taking over any concepts only seemingly demonstrated; and likewise to pseudo-questions which often are spread abroad as 'problems' for generations. (BT, p. 24/27–8)

I am not the first to point out how wildly unhelpful these remarks are, since they seem to provide no genuine contrast between phenomenology and any other form of inquiry. Is any discipline *not* 'opposed to all free-floating constructions' or 'pseudo-questions'? Heidegger himself seems to be aware of the potential emptiness of his remarks, when he follows them with an imagined rejoinder that this maxim 'expresses . . . the underlying principle of any scientific knowledge whatsoever'. Nonetheless, Heidegger wants to insist that there is a way in which phenomenology embodies this maxim distinctively, in contrast to the positive sciences: 'we are', Heidegger says, 'dealing with "something self-evident" which we want to get closer to' (BT, p. 24/28). Phenomenology's concern with what is manifest and with making things manifest or explicit marks it out as a fundamentally different kind of pursuit from any other kind of science or inquiry. Heidegger's etymological remarks aim to demonstrate this claim.

Etymologically, 'phenomenology' has two components, 'phenomenon' and 'logos', both of whose origins lie in ancient Greek and both of which concern the notion of manifestation (with 'phenomenon' emphasizing the showing side of manifestation, and 'logos' the seeing side). Taking them in order, as Heidegger does, 'phenomenon' derives from the Greek verb meaning 'to show itself'. Accordingly, 'the meaning of the expression "phenomenon" is *established as what shows itself in itself*, what is manifest' (BT, p. 25/28). Despite this seemingly straightforward formulation, Heidegger's subsequent discussion makes clear that the notion of something's *showing* itself requires considerable care, so as to avoid conflating it, as Heidegger claims many have, with other ideas, especially the notion of *appearance*.

The basic notion of something's showing itself admits of different possibilities, since something may show itself as what it is, but also as what it is *not*. The latter involves such notions as *seeming* and *semblance*. If, while sitting at my desk, I look out my study window across the front lawn, I may notice what I take to be a woodchuck coming out of its hole in the far corner. However, further inspection reveals that it is instead our fat old cat, Hamlet, who from a distance can easily be mistaken for a lumbering woodchuck. Here, something (our cat) shows itself, but as something it is not (a woodchuck): what I saw seemed for a moment to be a woodchuck, but was really a cat. Hamlet was manifest, but in a dissembling, deceptive way (though I don't want to suggest that our cat was *trying* to deceive me, performing imitations of a woodchuck, or any such thing). Heidegger observes that these two senses of something's showing itself (as what it is and as semblance) are 'structurally interconnected', by which he means that the very idea of showing brings with it the idea of something's showing itself as something other than what it really is. At the same time, Heidegger insists that the notion of something's showing itself as it is, rather than semblance or seeming, is the more 'primordial signification', since only something that *can* show itself can *seem* to be something else. Only because our cat, Hamlet, can show himself as what he is (a cat), can he also seem to be a woodchuck.

The basic idea of something's showing itself is thus the 'privileged' sense, while showing-as-semblance is a 'privative' modification. *Both* of these notions of showing are to be sharply distinguished from the idea of *appearance* (or worse, 'mere appearance'). Appearance does not involve the idea of something's showing itself, but instead means the *indication* of something that does not show itself. Heidegger uses the example of the relation between symptoms (fever, flushed cheeks, rash, etc.) and the underlying disease. The symptoms serve only to indicate the disease or, to put it differently, the disease announces itself by means of the symptoms, but does not show itself via them (either as what it is or as what it is not). But even this notion is not entirely divorced from the idea of showing: 'Although "appearing" is never a self-showing in the sense of phenomenon, appearing is possible only *on the basis* of a *self-showing* of something . . . Appearing is a *making itself known* through something that shows itself' (BT, p. 26/29). If we consider again the symptom–disease relationship, the symptoms are manifest, i.e. they show themselves, but as indicators of something that does not show itself.

However, the notion of appearance is even more complicated (or 'bewildering', to use Heidegger's term), than this first pass would suggest. Though Heidegger says that 'all indications, presentations, symptoms, and symbols have this fundamental formal structure of appearing, although they differ among themselves' (BT, p. 26/29), there are other senses that do not exemplify this 'basic formal structure'. In the example above, where I took our cat Hamlet to be a woodchuck, it is perfectly in order to say about that episode that, given the distance, Hamlet appeared to be a woodchuck, though it would be very odd to say that he was an indication, symptom or symbol of a woodchuck. Hamlet's presence did not announce the presence of an underlying woodchuck, nor did his presence stand for or represent a non-present woodchuck: he simply looked like, or seemed to be, a woodchuck. But 'appearance' need not connote any sense of semblance or misrecognition at all. If I say that Hamlet made an appearance at the water bowl last night or that he appeared before me this morning by leaping onto the bed, there is nothing in what I say that suggests anything illusory or indirect. To make matters worse, there is a more distinctively philosophical sense of 'appearance', where appearing is contrasted with what *never* shows itself. Here we have 'appearance' in the sense of 'mere appearance'. Though the appearance does genuinely show itself, it is never able to do anything more to announce or indicate something that is forever hidden from view, but not in a way that dissembles or misleads. Heidegger primarily has in mind here Kant's distinction between appearances and things-in-themselves.

That there is such a disparate variety of connotations bound up with the term 'appearance', ranging from indication to semblance to genuine self-showing, makes it a particularly poor candidate for cashing out the notion of a phenomenon. Heidegger therefore insists that we stick to the notion of a phenomenon as 'that which shows itself in itself'. Even this construal, though, admits of different interpretations. Heidegger distinguishes among what he calls the 'formal', 'ordinary' and 'phenomenological' conceptions of a phenomenon. The first of these may also be called a neutral conception, in that the notion of 'that which shows itself' is not further specified or qualified. The ordinary conception does add more specificity, construing what shows itself is as what is made available or manifest in ordinary (empirical) experience. Our cat Hamlet is a phenomenon in this sense, as is the woodchuck he resembles from a distance. Of course, Heidegger's interest lies primarily in the third, phenomenological conception, which, oddly perhaps, he first spells out by analogy with some key ideas in Kant's *Critique of Pure Reason*. (I say that this is odd both because a more direct explication would be welcome at this stage of Heidegger's account, but also because the Kantian apparatus of appearance, things-in-themselves and so on have already come in for criticism. It is thus strange immediately to invoke Kant more approvingly, albeit only by analogy.)

The invocation of Kant here works roughly like this: for Kant, appearances are the 'objects of empirical intuition'. Leaving aside their problematic characterization as appearances, they nonetheless satisfy the basic criteria of phenomena in the ordinary sense of the notion. Indeed, Heidegger himself uses the notion of 'empirical intuition' to explain what the ordinary conception of a phenomenon involves. Now Kant argues in the *Critique of Pure Reason* that *space* and *time* are the 'forms' of 'empirical intuition'. (They must be forms of intuition, rather than features of reality in and of itself, in order to explain the possibility of synthetic *a priori* judgements, but that's another story.) Everything that appears (that is an appearance) appears in space and time. More precisely, everything that appears does so at least in time (time is the form of both 'inner' and 'outer' intuition), while things that are objects of outer intuition appear in both space and time. Space and time are thus the 'conditions' objects or appearances must meet in order to *be* appearances, i.e. objects of empirical intuition. Anything that did not meet these conditions could never appear, and hence could never be a possible object of knowledge. Everything that shows itself in the ordinary sense is accompanied and made possible by space and time as their form; however, this 'accompaniment' is not usually 'thematic'. When I perceive the cup on my desk, I perceive it as spatially located and as spatially extended, indeed I must perceive it that way in order to perceive it at all; at the same time, I do not ordinarily attend to the space the cup is seen as inhabiting, nor do I give much thought to the features and characteristics space must have in and of itself. These non-thematic accompanying conditions of phenomena in the ordinary sense can, however, become thematic: space and time can become the explicit focus of my experience (when, for example, I do geometry), and thereby show themselves in themselves. Space and time, as the forms of intuition, are (analogues of) phenomena in the phenomenological sense: they accompany and make possible phenomena in the ordinary sense, but do so non-thematically. A phenomenology of space and time would treat them thematically, thereby allowing them to show themselves in themselves.

That phenomenology endeavours to make thematic what is otherwise non-thematic is apparent in the etymology of the '-ology' half of the term. Ordinarily, the suffix, '-ology', indicates the study or science of something or other (witness geology, biology, embryology, zoology and so on), but we have already seen that Heidegger denies that phenomenology has any special subject matter or domain of inquiry. Again, phenomenology is meant to designate a 'how' of inquiry, rather than a 'what'. Heidegger argues that if we attend to the original meaning of the term from which '-ology' derives, namely *logos*, this idea will become clearer. The Greek term *logos* is a richly textured term, replete with many philosophically heavy-duty connotations ('reason' and 'law' are sometimes used to translate it, for example, and it is the etymological source of the word, 'logic'). Heidegger claims that the basic signification of *logos* is 'discourse', where the basic signification of 'discourse' is 'letting something be seen'. We can get a sense of what Heidegger means here even if we consider what goes on in everyday conversation. Consider such mundane statements as, 'Hey, get a look at this', or, 'I bought milk yesterday', or, 'Here's my new car'. In all these cases, part of what is going on in saying them is that something is being brought to the attention of the person to whom the statements are addressed; something is being made manifest that may otherwise have gone unnoticed. (Of course, as with 'phenomenon', the possibility of letting something be seen is accompanied by the possibility of hiding something from view: discourse can obscure, sometimes deliberately as when someone lies or misleads, but also through less deliberate means, such as ignorance, confusion and misunderstanding.)

2C PHENOMENOLOGY AND ONTOLOGY

If we now put the terms together, we can say that phenomenology, as the *logos* of the *phenomena*, is the discourse of what shows itself, and so that phenomenology, in Heidegger's words, lets 'what shows itself be seen from itself, just as it shows itself from itself' (BT, p. 30/34). That formulation, however intricate, is still neutral among the ordinary, formal and phenomenological conceptions of phenomenology. However, if we consider again Heidegger's appeal to role of space and time in Kant's account of empirical intuition, we can get a feel for what the phenomenological sense of 'phenomenology' is supposed to be. In the first Introduction, Heidegger says early on that by 'being' is meant 'that which determines beings as beings, that in terms of which beings have always been understood' (BT, pp. 4–5/6). We can see in this formulation that it is precisely the notion of being that serves as the non-thematic accompanying condition of every entity that shows itself (just as space and time are, for Kant, the non-thematic accompanying conditions of the appearance of objects in empirical intuition). Being is always the being of an entity – every entity that is has some way of being – and every entity that Da-sein encounters is understood in its way of being, though not thematically or explicitly (recall our example involving squirrels and prime numbers). Thus, Heidegger declares: 'Phenomenology is the way of access to, and the demonstrative manner of determination of, what is to become the theme of ontology. *Ontology is possible only as phenomenology*' (BT, p. 31/35).

Heidegger's conception of phenomenology thus dovetails with his insistence on starting with Da-sein's understanding of being. The goal of phenomenology is to bring out what is implicit in that understanding by attending to Da-sein's encounters with entities, and that means working out or making explicit the *structure* of the understanding involved or operative in those encounters. Because of the pervasiveness of Da-sein's understanding of being, pretty much any and every encounter with entities is potentially revelatory. Hence, Heidegger's phenomenology is a phenomenology of 'everydayness'. The task is thus to show Da-sein 'as it is *initially and for the most part – in its average everydayness*' (BT, p. 15/16). Showing Da-sein in this way will allow for the exhibition of 'not arbitrary and accidental structures but essential ones' (BT, p. 15/16), and these will be structures pertaining both to Da-sein's way of being and to the entities that Da-sein encounters in its day-to-day affairs.

That Heidegger casts his concern as being with 'essential' rather than 'accidental' *structures* signals an affinity with Husserl's conception of phenomenology. Moreover, if we recall Husserl's interest in the notion of 'categorial intuition', we can further appreciate Heidegger's debt to Husserl, while also beginning to understand the way he transforms Husserl's conception of phenomenology. For Husserl, in categorial intuition or experience, the categories are both essential parts of that experience (without 'is' or 'being', as well as 'the', there could be no experience of seeing that the cup is white), and largely non-thematic (even when we see that the cup is white, the cup and the whiteness are at the centre of our attention, rather than 'the' and 'is'). One goal of phenomenology is to make these categorial dimensions explicit, so as to develop a worked-out account precisely of the categories. For Husserl, meeting this goal would establish the phenomenological basis of logic. Now, Heidegger takes over from Husserl the notion of categorial structure, but, in keeping with his conception of Da-sein's pre-ontological understanding of being as largely a matter of non-thematic ways of *acting*, he locates that categorial structure in Da-sein's encounters with entities, its everyday modes of engaging with, acting with and upon, entities. If phenomenology is to delineate more explicitly the categories that are operative in those categorially structured 'dealings' with entities, then, according to Heidegger, Husserl's phenomenological reduction cannot possibly be the right way to proceed. A reduction to the standpoint of 'pure consciousness' will, from Heidegger's perspective, screen off just what is most essential to making progress in phenomenology, namely those worldly encounters with entities whose being is understood by Da-sein. Being is 'that which determines beings as beings, that in terms of which beings have always been understood', which means that the categories are equally bound up with entities and Da-sein's understanding. Thus, any attempt to sever the connection to entities would efface that categorial structure.

Being is always the being of an entity *and* being is always what Da-sein understands, however implicitly, in its encounters with entities. For Heidegger, phenomenology cannot bracket or screen off the existence of those entities if it is to be the method of ontology. Heidegger still sometimes appeals to the notion of a phenomenological reduction, but his understanding of the notion is far different from Husserl's. This is especially evident in a passage from the opening of his *Basic Problems of Phenomenology* lectures, which were offered in close proximity to the publication of *Being and Time*. Heidegger writes:

> Apprehension of being, ontological investigation, always turns, at first and necessarily to some being; but then, *in a precise way, it is led away* from that being *and back to its being*. We call this basic component of phenomenological method – the leading back or reduction of investigative vision from a naively apprehended being to being – *phenomenological reduction*. We are thus adopting a central term of Husserl's phenomenology in its literal wording though not in its substantive intent. *For Husserl*, phenomeno-

logical reduction . . . is the method of leading phenomenological vision from the natural attitude of the human being whose life is involved in the world of things and persons back to the transcendental life of consciousness . . . *For us* phenomenological reduction means leading phenomenological vision back from the apprehension of a being, whatever may be the character of that apprehension, to the understanding of the being of this being. (BP, p. 21)

Heidegger's qualification in the last sentence – 'whatever may be the character of that apprehension' – is significant, as the modes of apprehension his phenomenology considers are Da-sein's everyday, *practical* encounters with entities. As a matter of practical engagement with entities, these encounters resist being construed as specifically phenomena of *consciousness*, and any attempt to isolate an episode of consciousness as what is essential to such encounters can only lead to distortion. (Despite its self-characterization as a work in phenomenology, it is striking how infrequently the word 'consciousness' appears throughout *Being and Time*.) Rather, the encounter must be taken whole. This means that the techniques associated with Husserl's conception of the phenomenological reduction (bracketing, purifying and so on) play no role in Heidegger's phenomenology; for Heidegger phenomenology leads 'investigative vision' from 'the apprehension of a being' back 'to the understanding of the being of this being' not by some ill-conceived attempt to purify that apprehension, but by *interpreting* it: 'From the investigation itself we shall see that the methodological meaning of phenomenological description is *interpretation*' (BT, p. 33/37). Thus: 'Phenomenology of Da-sein is *hermeneutics* in the original signification of that word, which designates the work of interpretation' (BT, p. 33/37).

In contrast (and in opposition) to Husserl's pure phenomenology, Heidegger proposes instead 'hermeneutic phenomenology', which proceeds by means of interpretation. That is, Heidegger's task is to describe Da-sein in its everydayness, but in a way that makes manifest the categorial structures that are operative there. A phenomenology of everydayness will not simply describe what Da-sein is doing, as though providing a running narration – that would be merely *ontical* description – but will delineate the *ontological* dimensions of that activity, i.e. make explicit the understanding of being at work in Da-sein's activity. As interpretation, Heidegger's phenomenology will lack the kind of final, absolute character of Husserlian phenomenology (Heidegger is happy to dispense as well with the kind of *certainty* Husserl thinks phenomenology can provide). Indeed, as *hermeneutical*, Heidegger's phenomenology is inherently *circular*, as it makes explicit what is implicit, which thereby affects what was until then implicit, which then requires further interpretation, and so on. We need to keep in mind that the phenomenological investigator, in this case Heidegger but the point applies more generally, is an 'instance' of Da-sein, whose being is at issue in the carrying out of this phenomenological project. It is not likely that the investigator's own understanding of being will remain unaffected by this philosophical pursuit.

Having laid out the basics of Heidegger's aims and methods, it would be best now to try to get a feel for how his interpretative project really works and what it reveals. Doing this will occupy us until the concluding sections of Part I. Though I will not be offering anything like a section-by-section commentary on *Being and Time* and will omit some topics (such as Da-sein's spatiality) altogether, I will follow the trajectory of Heidegger's discussion quite closely so that the reader can work back and forth between this guide and Heidegger's original work.

CHAPTER 3

BEING-IN-THE-WORLD: EQUIPMENT, PRACTICE AND SELF-UNDERSTANDING

The status of Da-sein's understanding of being as *pre-ontological*, as, in other words, implicit and operative in its activities rather than anything Da-sein may explicitly 'have in mind', dictates that a phenomenological investigation devoted to making the structures of that understanding explicit must be a phenomenology of everydayness. Another way to arrive at this same conclusion is to consider again the linkage for Heidegger between the idea that Da-sein has an understanding of being and that Da-sein is a being whose being is an issue for it: how things show up to Da-sein and how things matter to it are not two independent ideas for Heidegger, but are instead mutually sustaining notions. Phenomenology, if it is to proceed without falsification or distortion, must not try to pry these two notions apart. Heidegger repeatedly insists that the phenomenon he labels 'being-in-the-world' is a *unitary* phenomenon, which must be investigated without any kind of separation or fragmentation of its constitutive aspects.

3A 'ALWAYS ALREADY': DA-SEIN'S EVERYDAY ORIENTATION

From Heidegger's perspective, one of the great failures of Husserl's phenomenological reduction is the attempt to work out the structure of manifestation to consciousness in isolation from any engagement between consciousness and an environing world. For Husserl, any kind of commitment to, or belief in, the existence of the world is suspended or bracketed by means of the phenomenological reduction. For Heidegger, this attempt at suspension is doubly problematic. First, since the understanding of being is largely a matter of *worldly* activity, the world cannot be 'deleted' without thereby deleting precisely what phenomenology is in the business of investigating. This criticism of Husserl is again dictated by the linkage between the understanding of being and Da-sein's being being an issue for it, as well as by Heidegger's insistence that being is always the being of an entity and so Da-sein's understanding of being cannot be abstracted from its engagement with those entities it understands. The second criticism is slightly different, though it is connected to the 'non-thematic' character of Da-sein's understanding of being. That is, Heidegger rejects the phenomenological reduction not just for its misguided attempt to delete any commitment to, or belief in, the existence of the world, but also, more deeply, for portraying Da-sein's relation to the world precisely in terms of such notions as commitment and belief. The phenomenological reduction is meant to suspend what Husserl calls the 'natural attitude', his term for our everyday orientation in experience wherein we take for granted the existence of what we experience. In his *The History of the Concept of Time* lectures, Heidegger complains against Husserl that 'man's natural manner of experience ... cannot be called an attitude' (HCT, p. 113). This complaint is echoed in Division One of *Being and Time*, when Heidegger characterizes the initial target of a phenomenology of everydayness. Heidegger writes:

> But as an investigation of being it independently and explicitly brings about the understanding of being which always already belongs to Da-sein and is 'alive' in every association with beings. Phenomenologically pre-thematic beings, what is used and produced, become accessible when we put ourselves in the place of taking care of things in the world. *Strictly speaking, to talk of putting ourselves in the place of taking care is misleading. We do not first need to put ourselves in the place of this way of being in associating with and taking care of things.* Everyday Da-sein always already *is* in this way; for example, in opening the door, I use the doorknob. (BT, p. 63/67 – my emphasis)

The emphasized sentence may be read as directed against Husserl's characterization of our everyday orientation towards things as an attitude, since talk of attitudes implies that our everyday understanding is something that we may suspend and adopt. Heidegger's rejection here of the idea that we put ourselves into a position of concernfully dealing with entities is part and parcel of his rejection of the idea that we can shear off our relation to the world and still retain our understanding of being as a theme for phenomenological investigation. If concerning ourselves with entities were something we could put ourselves in a position to do, then it would also be something we could take ourselves out of a position to do. We could then study this attitude neutrally, as a set of beliefs and other commitments that we freely adopt and suspend. If Heidegger is right, however, about the proper way to characterize our pre-ontological understanding of being, then this kind of neutrality is neither desirable nor attainable. (Again, we can see why Heidegger proposes a hermeneutical phenomenology, since the method of interpretation proceeds without any pretence of neutrality.) Da-sein's involvement with the world, what Heidegger characterizes as Da-sein's 'being-in-the-world', cannot be considered as an optional 'add-on' to Da-sein, and so again not an attitude that Da-sein may adopt and suspend at will: 'being-in is not a "quality" which Da-sein sometimes has and sometimes does not have, *without* which it could *be* just as well as it could with it' (BT, p. 53/57).

Though I have been emphasizing the contrast between Heidegger and Husserl, it should be noted that Heidegger's insistence on the primacy of the notion of being-in-the-world registers more than just a local disagreement, a kind of intramural dispute among phenomenologists. For Heidegger, the historically more significant example of the kind of view he rejects is that of Descartes, the founding figure of modern Western philosophy. Consider Descartes' famous Method of Doubt and the subsequent discovery of the I, self or subject as surviving the doubt: the self can be vouchsafed as existing, even if all other beliefs (about the world, mathematics and even God) are suspended. Descartes' *cogito* is thus both epistemologically and ontologically significant: the self is first in the order of knowledge, since it can be known to exist even while everything else is open to doubt, and the self is revealed to be a special kind of entity, an immaterial being, that can exist apart from the goings-on of the material world. Heidegger rejects both the epistemological and ontological dimensions of Descartes' philosophy: 'One of our first tasks will be to show that the point of departure from an initially given *ego* and subject totally fails to see the phenomenal content of Da-sein' (BT, p. 43/46). There is a further, related aspect of Descartes' legacy that looms large in *Being and Time*: though for Descartes the Method of Doubt is devised and deployed only as tool to establish the order and structure of knowledge, he nonetheless is largely responsible for inaugurating modern philosophy's preoccupation with *scepticism*, i. e. with questions concerning the nature and possibility of the justification of one's beliefs. At the end of Division One, Heidegger takes up the issue of scepticism in order to expose its relation to distorted and, by that point in Division One, discredited conceptions of human existence.

Both *that* Da-sein understands things in their being and *how* Da-sein understands them are bound up with the way that Da-sein's own being is an issue for it. But the latter means that Da-sein confronts its existence as an *ongoing* concern, as, that is, something that it is always in the process of working out or determining, which means that Da-sein's existence essentially involves the idea of ongoing *activity*. Heidegger opens Division One by emphasizing just this idea about Da-sein: *'The "essence" of Da-sein lies in its existence'* (BT, p. 40/42). In its day-to-day activity, Da-sein is always 'taking a stand' on the kind of being it is, not in the sense of actively declaring itself to be one thing rather than another, but in engaging in some activities rather than others, taking up some tasks rather than others, adopting certain goals rather than others, and so on: 'It has somehow always already decided in which way Da-sein is always my own. The being which is concerned about in its being about its being is related to its being as its truest possibility. Da-sein *is* always its possibility' (BT, p. 40/42). Heidegger's appeal to *possibility* here is meant to underscore the way in which Da-sein's existence cannot be understood in the same terms that we use for other categories of entities. With the latter, notions like 'actuality', 'reality' and 'presence' are the key concepts: to be real is to be actual, which means being fully present at a particular time and place. As fully present, what is real is thus fully determinate as instantiating a particular slate of properties or characteristics. That Da-sein is to be understood in terms of its 'ownmost possibility' implies a displacement of these notions: Da-sein, as confronting and working out its existence, is *never* fully present or actual, and so is never determined by a slate of properties or features. Da-sein is always to be understood in terms of possibility, i. e. possible ways to be, which Da-sein is always taking up or leaving, choosing or ignoring, and so on. But 'possibility' in turn needs to be properly understood, since Heidegger's use in this context is different from standard uses of the term. That is, the notion of possibility is usually used in contrast to necessity and impossibility: to say that something is possible means that it is neither necessary nor impossible. To say that something is only possible usually means that it is not yet actual, but could be at some future time. If I look out the window and say, 'It might rain shortly', I'm talking about how things might be at a certain point in the future, in this case in the near future. At that later time, it either will be raining or it will not be, i. e. that possibility of rain will either be actualized or fail to be actualized. When Heidegger defines Da-sein in terms of possibility, we need to avoid this standard connotation of eventual actualization, as though Da-sein will someday fully be what it only possibly is now. All of Da-sein's defining characteristics are possibilities, which means that they are never fully actual or present, but instead ongoing, ever-developing ways of being. Da-sein is always 'pressing into possibilities', or, as Heidegger puts it, *projecting* itself in terms of various possibilities, various ways in which to be. Da-sein always *is* what it is 'on the way' to being. We will need to attend as well to Heidegger's talk of Da-sein in terms of its *ownmost* or *truest* possibility, since it is central to his development of the contrast between 'authenticity' and 'inauthenticity'. Much of Division Two of *Being and Time* is devoted to this contrast, though Heidegger alludes to it at the very beginning of Division One:

> And because Da-sein is always essentially its possibility, it *can* 'choose' itself in its being, it can win itself, it can lose itself, or it can never and only 'apparently' win itself. It can only have lost itself and it can only have not yet gained itself because it is essentially possible as authentic, that is, it belongs to itself. (BT, p. 40/42–3)

3B THE PROXIMITY OF USEFUL THINGS

How things show up or manifest themselves to Da-sein will largely be determined by the stand Da-sein takes on its existence: things will manifest themselves in ways that are coordinate with those activities, tasks and goals. Consider Heidegger's example of the workshop. For the carpenter whose workshop it is, the workshop is manifest as a familiar space, divided perhaps into different work areas and replete with an array of familiar tools (hammers, saws, screwdrivers, clamps and so on). That the workshop is manifest in this way, as a place for working with an array of tools that play various roles in that work, is conditioned by the carpenter's readiness to work in the workshop. Of course, there are other ways in which the workshop may manifest itself. Consider a pest inspector, who is called in to investigate possible termite damage. Though the inspector may notice the tools and so on, and notice them more or less *as* tools rather than just a bunch of stuff, the tools will largely be peripheral to the boards and beams that make up the workshop's structure. The inspector's readiness to search for termite damage dictates a different way in which the workshop shows itself. For yet someone else, who does not know the difference between, say, a jigsaw and a table-saw, the workshop may manifest itself as an odd, perhaps interesting, collection of tools, stuff for doing something or other but without any definite sense of just what.

A workshop is, of course, but one example, and is one that nowadays may not be readily accessible, at least for many of us. Further examples can be multiplied indefinitely. When I enter a classroom, how things show up is conditioned by my readiness to teach: the places the students and I occupy, the lectern, chalkboard and chalk, desks, chairs and so on, are all manifest in a way that is subordinate to the teaching of a class. When I enter my study with a readiness to write, my desk, books, computer and so on are all manifest in terms of whatever project I plan to work on (though various items might manifest themselves thereby as distractions from that project). We need not consider examples that are oriented around work or jobs, either. My kitchen is manifest to me in ways that are conditioned by my readiness to prepare a meal: sink, counters, refrigerator, oven, stove and utensils all show up in relation to the task of cooking. The field below my house is manifest as a good place to walk with my dog or explore with my children (and for the kayakers who frequent the field when the water is high, it shows up as a good place to put in for trips down the river).

If we begin to reflect on this ground-level phenomenology, Heidegger thinks that a number of significant results may already be discerned:

1. If we consider the *entities* that are manifest in our day-to-day activities, what shows up is what Heidegger calls *useful things* (*Zeug*, translated by Macquarrie and Robinson as *equipment*; useful things are *zuhanden*, which Stambaugh translates as 'handy', and Macquarrie and Robinson as 'ready-to-hand'). The basic characteristic of these entities is something-for-something (e.g. a

hammer for hammering, chalk for writing, a knife for chopping), which means that a useful thing shows up as having an 'assignment', or as having been assigned to play a role (or a variety of roles) in some particular task (or variety of tasks). In so characterizing what is manifest in everydayness, Heidegger thereby rejects as phenomenologically inadequate the idea that what shows itself is 'things' or 'mere things', what philosophers sometimes refer to as 'material objects'. Though Heidegger does have a story to tell about the manifestation of things as material objects – what he refers to as 'objective presence' (*Vorhandenheit*, translated as 'presence-at-hand' in Macquarrie and Robinson) in contrast to 'handiness' (*Zuhandenheit*, translated as 'readiness-to-hand' by Macquarrie and Robinson) – that story is very much secondary in relation to his account of readiness-to-hand. We thus need to be careful not to smuggle in a conception of things as material objects into the phenomenological account of useful things, as though the notion of a material object captures what these entities really are and their manifestation as useful is a kind of subjective 'colouration' of them:

> The kind of being of these beings is 'handiness'. But it must not be understood as a mere characteristic of interpretation, as if such 'aspects' were discursively forced upon 'beings' which we initially encounter, as if an initially objectively present world-stuff were 'subjectively colored' in this way. (BT, p. 67/71)

2. Useful things (equipment) are manifest in *circumspection*. While Husserlian phenomenology typically begins with perceptual experience, for example with an account of the structure of how things show themselves in visual experience, Heidegger argues that the manifestation of useful things must be understood in terms of the activities wherein they are put to use. Heidegger contends that 'the less we just stare at the thing called hammer, the more actively we use it, the more original our relation to it becomes and the more undisguisedly it is encountered as what it is, as a useful thing' (BT, p. 65/69). Rather than perceptual experience regarded in and of itself, which tends toward an account of how things look and can easily devolve into a phenomenology of staring, Heidegger refers to the 'sight' involved in dealings with equipment *circumspection*. In circumspection, one's dealings with particular tools and other items

of equipment are subordinate to the task in which they are employed, such that they are not the focus of one's ongoing experience at all: 'What is peculiar to what is initially at hand is that it withdraws, so to speak, in its character of handiness in order to be really handy' (BT, p. 65/69). In other words, the more smoothly and skilfully one engages with equipment, the less that equipment figures in one's awareness. A skilled typist, for example, barely notices the keys or even the screen on which the words are displayed; a skilled carpenter wields a hammer, all the while concentrating on the structure being built; most of us most of the time scarcely notice or feel our shoes as we walk.

We can see in Heidegger's account of circumspection his reconfiguration of Husserl's interest in categorial intuition. Things are indeed apprehended categorially in circumspection (as being handy, as being for hammering and so on), but the specific character of that apprehension cannot be understood on the model of the perceptual experience of an object and its properties. Instead, that categorial structure is operative implicitly in Da-sein's activities, in its taking hold of items of equipment and putting them to use. Da-sein relates to that categorial structure understandingly, but as pre-ontological, its understanding of those categorial structures is not something present to or in Da-sein as an 'intuition', i.e. as something present to consciousness. Rather, what is peculiar and primary about circumspective concern are the ways in which it eludes consciousness. Very often, when we try to call to mind what we do and how we do it in our navigation of our everyday roster of activities, we may find it difficult, if not impossible, to do. At the same time, our engagement in those activities is not something 'mindless' or unintelligent, let alone non-intentional. Instead, Heidegger wants to show how those largely unnoticed activities harbour a rich ontological–categorial structure, whose presence and primacy has been neglected by the entirety of the Western philosophical tradition, Husserl included.

Circumspection, for Heidegger, is not theoretical, not even implicitly: part of the upshot of his phenomenology of everydayness is a displacement of the notion of theorizing, such that it is a special, derivative way of engaging with the world. Da-sein's everyday engagement with equipment is not underwritten by an implicit theory, nor, Heidegger thinks, *can* it be. Our skilful engagement with equipment cannot be codified into various series of rules that might then be formally represented:

But we must realize that such formalizations level down the phenomena to the extent that the true phenomenal content gets lost . . . These 'relations' and 'relata' of the in-order-to, for-the-sake-of, the with-what of relevance resist any kind of mathematical functionalization in accordance with their phenomenal content. Nor are they something thought, something first posited in 'thinking,' but rather relations in which heedful circumspection as such already dwells. (BT, p. 82/88)

No matter what rules we formulate, even for such mundane tasks as hammering in a nail or downshifting on a car, there are at least three problems with the adequacy of any such rules. First, even if we could formulate rules, it does not follow that what we are doing when we act skilfully is really or implicitly (or subconsciously) following rules: the phenomenology of skilful engagement, wherein we non-reflectively take hold of equipment and put it to use, does not reveal any rules as part of the process. Second, any rules that we try to formulate will never fully capture the skill that is being modelled: our skilful engagement is too fine-grained and flexible to be captured by exceptionless rules. There would always need to be qualifications, *ceteris paribus* clauses and further specifications. Third and most devastatingly, no matter what rules one tries to formulate, following those rules requires that they be *understood*. But if understanding how to follow rules was itself a matter of following rules, a regress threatens (we would need rules for following rules, which in turn would need rules and so on). Even if there are some rules that we follow some of the time, understanding cannot be rules 'all the way down'.

3. Useful things are manifest in terms of a *totality*. Heidegger's equating of Husserlian phenomenology with a tendency toward 'staring' highlights the way in which Husserl's phenomenology treats as basic the perceptual experience of an isolated object. Indeed, the very idea of a material object implies a kind of unity and autonomy relative to whatever else there is: it is at least conceivable that reality were to consist of only one material object for all eternity. This is not the case with equipment: 'Strictly speaking, there "is" no such thing as *a* useful thing. There always belongs to the being of a useful thing a totality of useful things in which this useful thing can be what it is' (BT, p. 64/68). Every useful thing is what it is only insofar as it belongs to a 'totality of useful things'. A hammer is only a hammer

insofar as it belongs to a totality that includes such items of equipment as nails, lumber, saws and other tools and materials. 'The different kinds of "in-order-to" such as serviceability, helpfulness, usability, handiness, constitute a totality of useful things' (BT, p. 64/68). The significance of this claim is twofold: first, any totality of useful things is that particular totality only by being bound up with Da-sein's activities (the totality to which a hammer belongs is constituted by the 'in-order-to' of building, repairing, woodworking and so on), second, particular useful things are always manifest in terms of that totality: 'useful things always are *in terms of* their belonging to other useful things' (BT, p. 64/68).

4. The way of being of useful things is *relational*. That 'there "is" no such thing as *a* useful thing' means that every useful thing is what it is in virtue of its relations to other useful things, as well as the activities in which those items are caught up, and, finally, the kinds of self-understandings Da-sein's engaging in those activities express. To return again to the workshop and Heidegger's favourite example of a hammer, the following is a fragment of the series of relations that constitute what a hammer is:

A hammer = something <u>with-which</u> to hammer in nails <u>in-order-to</u> hold pieces of wood together <u>towards</u> the building of something <u>for-the-sake-of</u> Da-sein's self-understanding as a carpenter.

The underlined items in this formulation are what Heidegger calls 'referential' relations: every useful thing refers to other useful things (a hammer refers to nails and wood, for example), as well as activities and self-understandings. These relations are definitive of what any particular useful thing *is*, which is why Heidegger says that these relations are constitutive of the way of *being* of useful things. Something that was not caught up in this system of relations would not *be* a hammer, even if it were shaped exactly like a hammer and had the same material composition. Imagine discovering people living in some remote location who use hammer-shaped items only as weapons or as part of a game. In what sense would these things be hammers? We might say, 'Oh, they look just like hammers', but if we are being careful, we would not identify them as hammers.

Taken together, these four results intimate without yet making explicit the phenomenon of *world*. The significative structure of the 'referential totality', which is made possible by Da-sein's 'assigning itself' to that structure, is what Heidegger primarily means by world: 'We shall call this relational totality of signification *significance*. It is what constitutes the structure of the world, of that in which Da-sein as such always already is' (BT, p. 81/87). The last clause of this passage is especially important, as it emphasizes once again the ineliminability of the phenomenon of world with respect to Da-sein's way of being. Being-in-the-world is a 'unitary phenomenon', which means that we go wrong in trying to understand Da-sein and world as two independently intelligible notions that are somehow brought together or interact. The relational character of useful things helps to convey this unified character of being-in-the-world, as the several referential relations that constitute useful things relate variously to different useful things, as well as Da-sein's activities, purposes, goals and roles. All of these are thus mutually interdependent: no hammers without hammering, no hammering without building and no building without carpentry and the like. We can read these dependence relations as running the other way as well: the specific shape and character of carpentry is as dependent on hammers and hammering as these are dependent on carpentry.

It should be fairly clear by now that Heidegger's notion of world is not to be equated with the planet Earth or with the notion of the physical universe. However, Heidegger's use of the notion of world is not entirely novel or outlandish, as it accords with some ways in which the term is standardly used. Consider, for example, talk of particular worlds that are associated with different human pursuits: the business world, the world of academia and so on. Each of these have their characteristic activities, roles and goals, along with the various kinds of equipment that figure into them. The respective understandings of the participants in these worlds are likewise geared to those activities, roles and goals, along with the associated equipment. College professors tend to be comfortable on university campuses, teaching classes, publishing articles and books, attending conferences, talking shop with colleagues and so on. They by and large know their way about classrooms and libraries, syllabi and exams, and meetings with students and fellow faculty members. Often, professors do not feel 'at home' wearing business suits, gathering in executive boardrooms, having 'power lunches'. The trappings of business are largely unfamiliar to the average college professor, even if he or she has some inkling of what they are and how they generally work.

At the same time, these different worlds are not hermetically sealed units, such that participants in them are trapped within them without a sense of something beyond them. Worlds in the sense of the business world or the world of academia are really just sub-worlds (Heidegger characterizes them as 'special' worlds), parts of a larger public space of familiarity and intelligibility, and Heidegger is primarily interested in detailing the *structure* of this notion of world in general. This structure is what he refers to as the 'worldliness of the world'. All 'special worlds' partake of this general structure, and owing to this general structure, every special world is 'accessible' from any other, at least to some degree. Though the college professor and the business mogul may not feel an especially great affinity for each other, they can both make themselves understood to one another with respect to their particular pursuits and find a great deal of commonality and overlap in their overall ways of life (both may drive cars, shop in stores, have computers, speak English, eat at a table, use a fork and knife and so on). The issue of accessibility may become more pressing as the two special worlds are more temporally and geographically remote from one another: here the possibility of full comprehension may not be realizable, but even where it is not, the two worlds are still recognizable *as* worlds (I may not ever understand the ancient Mesopotamian world, and it may further be the case that no one from this point on ever will, but whatever glimpses the remnants of that culture afford make it clear that there was indeed a world there to be understood.)

Belonging to a world is most fundamentally a matter of what Heidegger calls *familiarity*: 'Da-sein is primordially familiar with that within which it understands itself in this way' (BT, p. 81/86). The 'in' in the locution, 'being-in-the-world', signifies this familiarity, this sense of feeling at home in a way of life. 'In' thus does *not* signify spatial containment, as though being-in-the-world primarily meant that Da-sein was always spatially located with respect to some larger, physically defined space. This may be true, but this notion of containment cannot capture or convey the sense of familiarity Heidegger is describing here. The physical world is one sense of 'world' (Heidegger lists four different senses of 'world' in § 14 of *Being and Time*), but we must be careful not to run together the notion of world in 'being-in-the-world' with the physical world, just as we must not run together the notion of equipment and that of a material object. Heidegger thinks that both philosophy and the natural sciences, especially since Descartes (though he thinks the problem goes all the way back to Parmenides), have tended to accord a privileged status to the material or physical world, such that everything else there *appears* to be must be rendered intelligible by means of the constellation of concepts associated with that privileged notion. Descartes, for example, thought that extension was the defining feature of the material world: to be materially real was to have some spatial dimensions. This claim may not be objectionable in and of itself, though there may be competing conceptions of what is materially or physically basic. What is problematic, from Heidegger's perspective, is the subsequent demand that *every* feature of what there is *either* be rendered intelligible in terms of extension *or* treated as a kind of subjective imposition onto what there is, a 'secondary property' of things that is best regarded as a feature of the mind's experience of the world. This is just the kind of 'subjective colouring' model that Heidegger wants to condemn as phenomenologically inadequate: both Da-sein's familiarity and what it is familiar with cannot be properly understood in terms of an essentially immaterial mind or subject interacting with essentially material objects. Such a problematic conception is symptomatic of philosophy's long-standing tendency to 'pass over' the phenomenon of world.

3C THE WORLD AS PHENOMENON

The tendency in philosophy to pass over the phenomenon of world begins in everydayness itself. We have seen already that the skilful use of familiar useful things involves the 'transparency' or 'withdrawal' of the equipment being used. When we are actively engaged, caught up in our task, we pay scant attention to the things we are using; we might be concentrating on the overall goal of our activity, but very often, we might be otherwise engaged in conversation, listening to music or just idly musing. Even more remote from our attention are the structural relations that obtain among useful things and connect them to our activities and pursuits: though we have some implicit grasp of these relations (we know, in some sense of 'know', that hammers are for hammering, though that may rarely, if ever, cross our minds), our grasp of them is 'non-thematic'. 'This familiarity with the world does not necessarily require a theoretical transparency of the relations constituting the world as world' (BT, p. 81/86). Again, Da-sein's pre-ontological understanding of being is not theoretical in nature, but instead a kind of taken-for-granted familiarity with the world. But just because this familiarity is taken for granted, it is scarcely noticed and so easy to miss. We might call this the 'paradox of proximity', in that we miss (and mis-describe) our everyday familiarity, along with the 'objects' of that familiarity, precisely because it is so close. 'True, Da-sein is ontically not only what is near or even nearest – we ourselves *are* it, each of us. Nevertheless, or precisely for this reason, it is ontologically what is farthest removed' (BT, p. 13/15). Da-sein's remoteness from itself ontologically and its tendency to miss or pass over the phenomenon of world are of a piece, since being-in-the-world is constitutive of Da-sein's ontological structure.

The world does, however, 'announce itself' in everydayness, and in more than one way. First, if we consider again the tendency of useful things to 'withdraw' when it is being skilfully deployed, we may notice that there are also times when this withdrawal is reversed. There are many occasions where what is usually handy is not: sometimes a needed tool may be missing, broken or simply in the way. In these situations, what is usually handy instead shows up as unhandy, and when this happens the useful thing in question comes to the fore of our attention. In such 'breakdown' situations, we now notice the useful thing and notice more explicitly just what it is *for*: 'But *in a disturbance of reference* – in being unusable for . . . – the reference becomes explicit' (BT, p. 70/74). Thus, breakdown situations serve to delineate more explicitly the kinds of referential relations that are constitutive of useful things. We need to be careful here, however, since Heidegger is not saying that every time my pen malfunctions or I cannot find my keys, I then gain insight into the underlying ontology of useful things: the assignment 'does not yet become explicit as an ontological structure, but ontically for our circumspection which gets annoyed by the damaged tool' (BT, p. 70/74). We have here only the beginnings of what a phenomenology of everydayness renders more explicit. In breakdowns, 'the context of useful things appears not as a totality never seen before, but as a totality that has continually been seen beforehand in our circumspection. But with this totality the world makes itself known' (BT, p. 70/75). The world may announce itself in these situations, but most of the time, the breakdown is so temporary that Da-sein simply resumes its circumspective activity almost immediately.

A second way in which the phenomenon of world comes into view is via a special kind of useful thing that Heidegger considers under the general heading of *signs*. We have seen already that the way of being of useful things is relational in nature: what it is to be any useful thing involves its being caught up in myriad relations. These relations are *referential* relations, and so every useful thing refers, variously, to other useful things, activities, projects, goals and roles. However, the notion of reference here is markedly different from the referential character of signs. Consider the difference between a hammer, which, as a hammer, refers to, among other things, nails and a sign at the local hardware store that reads, 'Nails: Aisle 3'. Both the hammer and the sign refer to nails, but in very different ways. Heidegger explains the difference by saying that the sign *indicates* nails, whereas the hammer does not. While what it is to be a hammer is constituted in part by its relation to nails, the hammer does not point to, or draw our attention towards, nails; any such relations are only tacitly grasped in our ongoing circumspective engagement with the hammer. Indeed, in the carpenter's ongoing activity in his workshop, neither the hammer nor the nails need occupy his attention to any great degree; again, this is part and parcel of useful things' general tendency to withdraw. Things are different in the case of signs, since the whole point of a sign is to be noticed so that it might direct our attention in one direction or another. (A sign that no one noticed would be a very poor sign indeed.) Signs work by indicating something or other, and indication only succeeds insofar as the sign engages our attention. Signs 'let what is at hand be encountered, more precisely, let their context become accessible in such a way that heedful association gets and secures an orientation' (BT, p. 74/79–80). Signs, by orienting our dealings, light up a particular region of the world, allowing it to be noticed more explicitly. A sign *'explicitly brings a totality of useful things to circumspection so that the worldly character of what is at hand makes itself known at the same time'* (BT, p. 74/80). Signs thus have a kind of revelatory function, and so serve to make things 'conspicuous'.

3D THE PRIORITY OF USEFUL THINGS

Disruptions in the referential totality can serve to bring structural aspects of that totality into view: in breakdown situations, the world 'announces itself'. Such disruptions may also be revelatory in another way. Rather than directing our attention towards the world and its constitutive structural relations, what can show itself in breakdowns is what Heidegger calls the 'objectively present' (or present-at-hand), his name for what might otherwise be called 'mere things' or 'stuff'. In a breakdown situation, what shows up may be something unhandy, but if circumspection is sufficiently disrupted so that we succumb to almost passive staring, we may begin to view what before showed up as handy as only objectively present: 'As a deficient mode of taking care of things, the helpless way in which we stand before it discovers the mere objective presence of what is at hand' (BT, p. 69/73). We may begin to view what stands before us as a mere, rather than useful, thing, something with properties and characteristics in and of itself, rather than as something for various tasks or projects. Consider here the difference between noting of a hammer that it is too heavy for a particular task and recording its weight. The latter is true of the hammer regardless of its constitutive referential relations, whereas it can only be too heavy (or too light) relative to a situation where it is to be put to use.

Seeing what there is as only objectively present is not an illegitimate way of seeing, according to Heidegger. Indeed, the revelation of objective presence is just that, a revelation of something genuinely there. Where Heidegger balks is at the suggestion that this revelation is of something more primary or basic than handiness. What fosters this suggestion is the observation that ' "there are" handy things, after all, only on the basis of what is objectively present' (BT, p. 67/71). There is certainly something right about this observation: if one were to destroy the material object that was revealed when circumspective engagement with the hammer ceased, that would certainly be the end of the hammer as well. What Heidegger wants to reject is the further implication that 'handiness is ontologically founded in objective presence' (BT, p. 67/71). That would only follow if one could make sense of, or understand, what it is for something to be a useful thing on the basis of what it is for something to be merely objectively present, and Heidegger contends that this cannot be done: § 21 of *Being and Time*, which focuses on Descartes' conception of material substance, contains a lengthy argument to this effect. Heidegger's argument turns on the mismatch between handiness and objective presence: useful things always to be understood in terms of a *totality*, bound together by a network of referential relations, whereas what is objectively present consists of at least conceptually, if not causally, independent objects and properties. If one starts with what is objectively present, the challenge is one of how to get to the thing of use from there. How, that is, is one to account for the various constitutive features of useful things, when one's resources are so thoroughly different? There do not, after all, appear to be anything at all like referential relations in what is purely objectively present. Heidegger argues that often such accounting involves gross distortions of useful things by treating them as objectively present things that have been somehow 'invested with value'. The problem with any such manoeuvre is twofold: first, since the process of 'investment' must be piecemeal, this way of founding things of use overlooks the way that being handy involves a *totality*. Secondly, the very notion of 'investment' is itself obscure, since it is unclear where to locate such a process of investment or to whom it should be ascribed. (Recall Heidegger's rejection of the idea that our circumspective dealings with what is useful involve our 'putting ourselves in the place of taking care'. We do not first need to put ourselves in the place of this way of being in associating with and taking care of things. This rejection means that there is room for a process of investing what shows up as only objectively present with value.) Ultimately, Heidegger argues that the attempt to 'reconstruct' useful things on the basis of what is only objectively present faces a dilemma: either such a project must presuppose an understanding of useful things (and so fail to ground what is useful ontologically in what is objectively present) *or* it must proceed blindly (and so again fail in the task of ontological grounding). This dilemma is implicit in the following pair of questions raised by Heidegger at the culmination of his critique of Descartes:

> And does not this reconstruction of the initially 'stripped' thing of use always need the *previous, positive view of the phenomenon whose totality is to be reestablished in the reconstruction*? But if its ownmost constitution of being of the phenomenon is not adequately explicated, are we not building the reconstruction without a plan? (BT, p. 92/99)

Of course, Heidegger rejects the supposition that serves as the basis for the entire reconstructive enterprise, namely that the 'thing of use' first shows itself to us 'stripped'. The phenomenology of everydayness is committed instead to the idea that how things show up is 'always already' as useful things. Da-sein does not first take in, perceptually or otherwise, mere objects, objectively present stuff, which it then imbues (or 'colours') with some kind of functional value or significance. Significance is the primary phenomenon, rather than something built up or derived from a more austere apprehension of what there is. Heidegger thus claims that the apprehension of a significant world, understood as an array of useful things, purposes, projects, roles and goals, is not the achievement of an isolated *subject* confronting a world of *objects*; rather, everyday Da-sein and the everyday world are co-original (or 'equiprimordial') manifestations, mutually informing and sustaining one another. As such, Heidegger rejects the conceit that the everyday world is merely a kind of subjective appearance. Though it is true that the everyday world cannot be regarded as fully objective, what would show up in a 'view from nowhere', that observation alone does not relegate the everyday world to the category of mere appearance: '*Handiness is the ontological categorial definition of beings as they are "in themselves"*' (BT, p. 67/71). Thus, we need to be careful not to read 'not fully objective' as tantamount to 'subjective'. Instead, we need to see Heidegger here as trying to break the grip of these two categories – subjective and objective – as marking out the only two possibilities. Everyday Da-sein and the everyday world cannot be adequately or properly interpreted in the terms provided by these two categories, and so Heidegger thinks we are better off avoiding them altogether. (This is not to say that Heidegger has no place in his phenomenology for talk of subjects and objects, but such talk occupies a decidedly secondary position, derived from the phenomena of everydayness that are best described without it.)

3E THE ANONYMITY OF EVERYDAYNESS

Despite Heidegger's admonitions and protestations concerning the subject–object distinction, there may still be a lingering sense that his phenomenology of everydayness is largely a characterization of how things are subjectively apprehended. If we consider again even our sketch of how the workshop is manifest, were not the variations in the way it was manifest keyed to the individuals who encountered it? The workshop shows up *as* an array of tools ready for use *to* the carpenter whose shop it is, whereas it shows up differently *to* the termite inspector, and differently again to someone wholly devoid of the skills had by the carpenter. While this kind of variety or relativity must be acknowledged, nonetheless we should not take it as indicative of the subjective character of manifestation. A number of considerations tell against taking this relativity as pointing in this direction. To begin with, the ways in which the workshop is manifest to our various individuals are not entirely disparate or unrelated. There is instead considerable overlap among them, and so the differences are more ones of emphasis. The carpenter's readiness is geared to the tools, whereas the termite inspector's is geared to the beams and boards making up the structure of the workshop, but this does not mean that each readiness thoroughly effaces what is manifest from the perspective of the other. Indeed, if we consider again our remarks on the accessibility of one world from another, here is a pretty easy case of it: the carpenter, the termite inspector and the carpentry novice can all coordinate and convey their respective understandings. More importantly, that coordination and conveyance will be facilitated by the workshop itself. When the carpenter tells the inspector that he will move his workbench away from the wall, the workbench and its contents will be equally manifest to both of them; similarly, the inspector can call the carpenter's attention to a particular post or beam, indicating to him some worrisome patterns of wear in the wood. Finally, the carpenter can instruct the novice, showing him which tools are which, what they are for and how they are used, thereby enriching the novice's apprehension of the workshop by equipping him with a readiness to engage skilfully with it. In considering the interactions among these three individuals, we do not find ourselves needing to multiply entities, as though the hammer as it shows itself to each of them were something different in each case, nor do we need to add 'appearances' to the workshop understood as a totality of interrelated equipment.

We can further dispel the aura of subjectivity even if we restrict our attention to just the carpenter's encounter with the workshop. Even if the workshop is his own private shop, used by him alone without partners or assistants, the manifestation to him of the workshop is nonetheless inflected by features and relations that point beyond the carpenter, understood as an isolated subject or agent.

That is, many, if not all, of the basic relations of the referential structure making up the workshop will not make any special reference to the carpenter personally, even if, again, the tools are his tools alone. The hammer is manifest as something for hammering, the saw as for sawing and so on, but that 'for hammering' and 'for sawing' do not carry any kind of personalized specification. Rather, the 'for hammering' and the like designate how the hammer and other tools are to be used by *anyone* at all. These designations are not something the carpenter himself imposed or decided, except in those cases perhaps where he has customized his tools or rigged up some new kind of equipment, but even these latter designations wear a cloak of anonymity. The hammer's showing itself as a hammer is not up to the carpenter; indeed, what it is to be a hammer is not based in any kind of individual decision or imposition. Relations that are both anonymous and normative, i.e. relations specifying how anyone *ought* to use it, constitute the hammer, along with other items of equipment. Heidegger refers to this anonymous, normative character of everydayness as '*das Man*', which is translated rather unhelpfully in both Stambaugh and the Macquarrie and Robinson edition of *Being and Time* as 'the "they"'. The word '*man*' in German usually means 'one', as in 'One says . . .', and so is meant to be inclusive. If I say, 'One hammers with a hammer', that is as applicable to me as it is to my interlocutor. 'The "they"', on the other hand, does not carry these inclusive connotations. Were I to say instead 'They hammer with hammers', then I am holding that use at arm's length, identifying it neither with my understanding of hammers, nor really even my interlocutor's. (There is nonetheless a dark side to Heidegger's appeal to *das Man*, which the extant translations serve to emphasize. We will consider that aspect of *das Man* shortly.)

Useful things, along with the rest of the everyday world, are thus constituted by a kind of anonymous understanding, available to anyone and everyone whose world it is. Da-sein's everyday existence is thus bound up not just with useful things, projects and purposes, but with *others* as well. As being-in-the-world, Da-sein's way of being equally involves what Heidegger calls, 'being-with', which indicates the way in which Da-sein's existence involves an understanding of others (i.e. other Da-seins). Indeed, even using the locution, 'others', can be misleading, if it suggests any kind of essential separation: ' "The others" does not mean everybody else but me –

those from whom the I distinguishes itself. They are, rather, those from whom one mostly does *not* distinguish oneself, those among whom one is, too' (BT, p. 111/118). Da-sein's encounters with others are marked by what Heidegger calls *solicitude*, in contrast to the *concern* that characterizes its circumspective engagement with useful things. The difference in terminology indicates the difference in understanding involved in each range of encounters. Other Da-seins are encountered as categorically distinct from items of useful things (and, of course, mere objects), which means that they show themselves in terms that are inapplicable to other kinds of entities. This is already evident in the idea that other Da-seins show themselves as having the same way of being as the Da-sein to whom they are manifest, but we can see it more concretely if we consider some of the ways we are present to one another. For example, we generally take account of one another in ways that we never take account of anything else – the appearance of another person may mark an opportunity for greeting, conversing, joking, sympathizing, commiserating, ignoring, insulting, debating, arguing, raging, flirting, seducing and so on. None of these possibilities is truly or fully available in Da-sein's encounters with other kinds of entities. (They may be so to a limited degree in our encounters with at least some kinds of animals, but we need to recall that Heidegger insists upon a sharp distinction between our way of being and that belonging to animals.)

Heidegger's characterization of the everyday world as essentially involving being-with and *das Man* – '*Das Man* itself articulates the referential context of significance' (BT, p. 121/129) – underscores its *public* character. The everyday world is a public world, within which everyday Da-sein orients itself in a public, common manner. Indeed, for Heidegger, *das Man* is the answer to the question of the 'who' of everyday Da-sein: 'The self of everyday Dasein is the *Man-self* which we distinguish from the *authentic self*, the self which has explicitly grasped itself' (BT, p. 121/129). The distinction Heidegger draws here is indicative of what I referred to previously as the 'dark side' of his account of *das Man*. Though Heidegger labels *das Man* a 'primordial phenomenon', and insists that it thus 'belongs to Da-sein's positive constitution', at the same time it also contributes to Da-sein's alienation from itself (here we see the merits of the standard translation, in that 'the "they"' emphasizes the alienating tendencies of everyday life). How can Heidegger have it both ways here? This last question has proven vexing to readers of Heidegger, and has sparked a number of intramural debates in the Heidegger literature. Without trying to dismiss these debates and the complexity of the matters at issue, let me try to suggest an answer. In everydayness, Da-sein is caught up in a world structured according to anonymous norms. These norms are pervasive, manifest at least implicitly wherever something is manifest as something to be used, to be done and to be said. There is certainly something unobjectionable, even 'positive', about these pervasive norms, in the sense that their deletion would thereby delete the very possibility of anything being manifest as something to be used, done or said. That is, it is not at all clear how things would be manifest without these norms, nor is it clear how anything like them could be established on the basis of some other form of manifestation. We have seen already that Heidegger rejects the idea of useful things being 'rebuilt' from the apprehension of what is objectively present, and his argument on that front is relevant here. If we imagine a subject of experience who encounters an environment devoid of the significance Heidegger describes, it is not clear how to characterize that experience, nor what that experience would allow. What in this subject's experience would allow for the idea that what is manifest to it is *for* something, that something has a use, or any practical significance at all? If we try to imagine this subject labelling bits and pieces of its environment with various 'use-tags', so as to designate that some things are for some tasks and other things are for others, we still need to know how this subject understands what being-for-something *means* in all these cases. Having a use or purpose is more than just having a label affixed; any such label must be underwritten by a grasp of what something's being for something is all about, and that, Heidegger contends, involves precisely the kind of anonymous normative structure he's described. The very idea of something's being for something is an *impersonal* designation, and so the very idea of something's having a use involves this kind of impersonal articulation. Our imagined subject, if it is to have a grasp of what something is for, must have this kind of impersonal perspective, a grip, at least implicitly, on the idea of an anonymously articulated norm. Again, Heidegger's argument is that any such grasp cannot be built up out of, or account for on the basis of, anything described in more austere terms. Hence, the idea that *das Man* is something positive.

At the same time, to be caught up in this anonymous normative structure is to experience a kind of 'pull' to conform to it. The very idea of a norm dictates how something *ought* to be used, done or said, and that the norms constitutive of everydayness are both pervasive and anonymous means that everyday Da-sein experiences them as binding pretty much everywhere all the time. There is thus a constant tendency to measure oneself against others (Heidegger calls this 'distantiality'), gravitate towards a common way of doing things ('averageness'), and so efface anything unique, genuine or even different ('levelling'). Consider the perils of popularity and the charge levelled at various kinds of artists (musicians, writers, painters, etc.) of 'selling out'. The force of the charge is that by creating something for a larger number of people, the artist will thereby water down her creation so that it will be readily available for that larger number (just think about how many bands go downhill once they've signed to a major label). The problem here is not so much a matter of numbers, as though there were a tipping point that could be quantitatively determined. (The problem is sometimes treated this way by those who fetishize the overly rare or obscure, such as members of college radio stations who prize seven-inch vinyl pressings in the low three-figures.) Instead, for Heidegger, the problem lies in the way things circulate at further and further remove from their 'sources' (and this is more likely to happen as greater and greater numbers of people are involved).

That things can be repeated, passed along and circulated is essential to the kind of everyday intelligibility Da-sein moves within (what would it be like if what I said could not be repeated by someone else?), but these processes bring with them the danger of dilution, i.e. the danger that what will be passed on will be only the barest outline of the original, devoid of the understanding that informed it. Consider, as an example, a neighbour's extolling the virtues of the rack-and-pinion steering on his new car. Now in some sense, the neighbour's use of the words 'rack-and-pinion' is in order; for example, he applies it to the steering of the car, rather than the brakes, and to the car, rather than his bedroom closet or kitchen sink. At the same time, there is likely to be something impoverished about his use of the words, since it is very likely that he has little to no real understanding of what rack-and-pinion steering really *is*. He may have picked up the terminology from his car dealer or from the sales brochure, heard about it on CarTalk, or from a friend who reads lots of magazines for auto aficionados. If the neighbour picked it up from the dealer, he too may have a pretty impoverished understanding as well: it may be little more than a 'talking point' handed out in a sales class or something that he too picked up from the brochure. The neighbour and the car dealer are guilty of what Heidegger refers to as 'idle talk', though again he counsels that this need not be a pejorative designation: anything that has a meaning must at the same time be transmittable as idle talk (here again we see the positive and the negative bound together). The term 'rack-and-pinion' can be endlessly circulated, which is essential to its having a meaning, but such endless circulation can be cut off or detached from any real grasp of that meaning. In contrast to the neighbour and the dealer, consider the words as they are said by an automotive engineer or mechanic: present here is a kind of genuine understanding, a real sense of what these terms designate, that was lacking in the other occasions of use.

While Heidegger is interested in this notion of genuine meaning in a general sense, his primary concern is with this kind of genuine understanding of one's own existence: the pull towards conformity that is part and parcel of everyday existence instils in Da-sein a *Man*-self, thereby obscuring from view the possibility of Da-sein's own authenticity. Recall the paradox of proximity and the principal illustrations of that paradox: 'True, Da-sein is ontically not only what is near or even nearest – we ourselves *are* it, each of us. Nevertheless, or precisely for this reason, it is ontologically what is farthest removed' (BT, p. 13/15). What this suggests is that Da-sein is most prone to idle talk, to circulate things divorced from their genuine source, when the 'source' in question is precisely Da-sein's own existence. Da-sein's talk idles to the greatest degree when the 'subject' of that talk is Da-sein itself.

The perils of everydayness may be discerned from yet another perspective. Consider again the kind of transparency that attends our everyday skilful activity: just as useful things have a tendency to 'withdraw' in that activity, so too is Da-sein wholly absorbed in and by the task. This kind of absorption ramifies throughout Da-sein's everyday existence, such that Heidegger characterizes everyday Da-sein as *dispersed*:

This dispersion characterizes the 'subject' of the kind of being which we know as heedful absorption in the world nearest encountered. If *Da-sein* is familiar with itself as the *Man*-self, this also means that *das Man* prescribes the nearest interpretation of the world and of being-in-the-world. (BT, p. 121/129)

Absorbed in its everyday routines, dispersed into its various concerns, Da-sein is thereby remote from itself, such that the distinctive character of its own existence is screened off from it. We can become so enmeshed in our day-to-day activities that we end up leading lives whose shape and character are a mystery to us, in the sense that we may be unable to account for just how our lives ended up looking this way. We may find ourselves struck by the question, 'Just how did I get to this point, where my life looks like *this*?' Worse still, we may not even get so far as being struck by such a question at all, so thorough is the extent of our dispersal. Our lives may, in other words, consist of little more than a series of distractions, a tumult of activities one after the other, without any pause for reflective evaluation. Something is needed to shake us out of this pattern of absorption and distraction, and the transition from Division One to Division Two is largely a matter of documenting the nature and possibility of this special 'something'. Before examining this all-important transition, there are several features of Division One that need to be considered.

CHAPTER 4

THE CARE-STRUCTURE

By the end of Chapter IV of Division One of *Being and Time*, Heidegger's phenomenology of everydayness has progressed to the point where he has given an account of the *world* as it is manifest in Da-sein's everyday activity, starting from those entities-within-the-world that are caught up in Da-sein's day-to-day routines (useful things). In doing so, he has at the same time offered a critique of standard philosophical (and scientific) accounts of reality, which try to explain or account for what there is primarily, and sometimes even exclusively, in terms of what is objectively present. He has, moreover, provided an answer to the 'who' of everyday Da-sein, via his account of the fundamental constitutive role of *das Man*, the anonymous yet authoritative normative structuring of the 'referential totality'. All the while, Heidegger insists on the *unitary* character of the 'structures' he has been explicating. Though different aspects have been the focus at different points in his discussion, Heidegger warns against 'any disruption and fragmentation of the unitary phenomenon' (BT, p. 123/131). Accordingly, Heidegger circles back in Chapter V to the first part of his preliminary formulation of Da-sein's way of being, being-in-the-world. That first part – being-in – had been given a preliminary characterization at the outset of Division One by means of the distinction between familiarity and mere spatial containment. (Heidegger also explains early on why Da-sein's basic familiarity with the world should not be understood in terms of *knowledge*. Instead, he argues that knowledge is a 'founded mode' of being-in-the-world, which means that knowledge is based upon a more fundamental form of familiarity, viz. engaged, non-theoretical circumspective concern. I will return shortly to Heidegger's concerns about knowledge and its often philosophically problematic character.)

Rather than a new topic, then, Chapter V is offered as a 'more penetrating' consideration of one already on the table, so as to 'get a new and more certain phenomenological view of the structural totality of being-in-the-world' (BT, p. 123/131). Indeed, the discussion of Chapter V is meant to be preparatory for an account of the 'primordial being of Da-sein itself, care' (BT, p. 123/131). All of the structures delineated in Division One provisionally in the service of the notion of being-in-the-world are thus meant to find a more completed articulation within the idea of *care*, as contributions to the *care-structure*. (For reasons we will consider later, Heidegger contends that even the seemingly full disclosure of the care-structure at the close of Division One is still importantly provisional and incomplete.) There should be little that is surprising about Heidegger's appeal to care at this point in the text, as the idea is meant to gather together and make more explicit a number of ideas that have been circulating since the opening sections of *Being and Time*. That is, we have been told that Da-sein is a being whose being is an *issue* for it, that Da-sein is a being for whom things *matter*, that Da-sein's everyday activity is marked by various modes of *concern* for the tasks in which it is engaged and by various modes of *solicitude* for the others whom it encounters. The appeal to care is even less surprising in the original German, owing to the etymological connections among care (*Sorge*), concern (*Besorgen*) and solicitude (*Fürsorge*), which are lost in translation. Care thus serves as an umbrella term that provides a kind of structural unity for all these aspects of Da-sein's existence. Again, we can see the way in which Heidegger should not be understood as adducing further features of Da-sein's way of being as he proceeds through Division One. Just as, at the very beginning, the ideas that Da-sein is a being whose being is an issue and that Da-sein is a being with an understanding of being are not, upon closer scrutiny, two separate ideas, so too are the further formulations not so much new facts or features, but further explications of those original ideas. Heidegger is thus being true to his conception of phenomenological method as *interpretation*, in that renewed attention to the phenomenon of being-in-the-world results in an ever-deepening interpretation, while all the while focused precisely on that one phenomenon.

For all its strategic importance, Chapter V is a rather unruly chapter, containing numerous discussions – of discourse, interpretation and assertion, for example – that do not contribute directly to the goal of explicating the care-structure. This is not to say that these discussions are mere digressions or in any way superfluous. In many ways, they discharge debts that Heidegger has accrued by this point in the work. For example, his claim in the second Introduction that the proper method of phenomenology is interpretation was entered without much discussion of just what 'interpretation' is supposed to mean; § 32 in Chapter V supplies that further discussion. Heidegger's introduction of the notion of *discourse*, along with its principal manifestation in *language*, also fills a kind of gap, since it is hard to imagine most, if not all, of the everyday 'dealings' described previously in Division One being carried on in an entirely mute fashion: Da-sein's engagement with the world and with others in everydayness would seem instead to be pervaded by language. It is not clear, however, just where to place discourse and language in the overall economy Heidegger elaborates in Chapter V: his claim that discourse is 'equiprimordial' with the other structural aspects of being-in explored in the chapter disrupts the threefold articulation of being-in he elaborates. (That the structure is threefold is no accident for Heidegger, but intimates the ways in which this structure is ultimately to be interpreted in terms of *time*. Adding a fourth aspect to the structure only serves to obscure that intimation.)

4A THROWNNESS AND PROJECTION

We will concentrate primarily on trying to work out the care-structure. To do so, I propose working backwards from the opening sections of Chapter VI, where Heidegger at last offers a formulation of the care-structure. With that formulation in hand, we can then explore each of its constitutive aspects. We will also need to consider the peculiar ordering of these aspects, as this too tells us something significant about Da-sein's way of being. The formulation Heidegger offers reads as follows:

> The being of Da-sein means being-ahead-of-oneself-already-in (the-world) as being-together-with (innerworldly beings encountered). (BT, pp. 179–80/192)

The formulation that appears after 'means' divides into three constitutive aspects: ahead-of-itself; being-already-in; and being-alongside. Let us consider each of these in turn.

That Da-sein is 'ahead-of-oneself' is signalled already by the claim that Da-sein is a being whose being is an issue for it. As an issue for it, Da-sein's way of being is an *ongoing* concern, something that it is constantly taking a stand on and determining. Thus, Da-sein is always on the way to being what it is, and so is always characterized by a 'not yet'. We see these ideas at work in Heidegger's claim that Da-sein is always to be understood in terms of *possibility*, rather than actuality. Again, though, we need to bear in mind Heidegger's technical rendering of the notion of possibility as applied to Da-sein's way of being, since it should not be understood as referring to some future actuality that Da-sein will eventually realize or inhabit. Da-sein *is* its possibilities, which means that Da-sein is always engaged in its *current* activities 'for-the-sake-of' one or several ongoing ways to be. In Chapter V of Division One of *Being and Time*, Heidegger refers to this idea of Da-sein's being-ahead-of-itself as *understanding*, which in turn he explicates in terms of *projection*. Da-sein is always 'projecting itself' or 'pressing into possibilities', which again signifies the way Da-sein's ongoing activity has a kind of ineliminable futural dimension. The 'for-the-sake-of' always points beyond what is currently actual, since what exactly that is can only be cashed out with reference to the possibilities Da-sein is projecting.

Of course, Da-sein's self-projection does not stand alone. Recall once again Heidegger's rejection of the idea that we need to 'put ourselves into a position to concern ourselves' with what is available as useful in everydayness. Da-sein is 'always already' situated in some ongoing, publicly intelligible nexus of activity, and the second aspect of Heidegger's formulation (being-already-in (the world)) is meant to capture this sense that Da-sein's projection is always on the basis of some already-given orientation. This aspect of Da-sein's way of being is dubbed by Heidegger '*Befindlichkeit*', which has no ready translation into English. Stambaugh translates the term as 'attunement', Macquarrie and Robinson translate it as 'state of mind', which is an especially unfortunate choice as it suggests that *Befindlichkeit* is primarily a matter of what one thinks or believes. Other translations have been proposed, such as 'predisposedness', and 'situatedness'. None of these is ideal, as none of them captures the contributing terms in Heidegger's coinage. The term is based upon a common German question, one of the first learned in any elementary German class: 'Wie befinden Sie sich?' The question, translated verbatim, means, 'How do you find yourself?' More smoothly, the question asks in a polite form how one is doing, or, less formally, 'How's it going?' The verbatim translation, clunky though it is, retains the notion of *finding*, which is useful for making sense of Heidegger's coined term. *Befindlichkeit* denotes the condition of Dasein as always *finding itself* in a world whose principal contours are not of its own choosing *and* as oriented towards that world in a manner that it likewise has little control over. At the broadest level, we can see *Befindlichkeit* at work in the myriad ways the referential totality shows itself with its constitutive relations already in place: I do not, and never did, choose what pens and pencils are for, how hammers and screwdrivers are used, what role the colander and the kettle play in the kitchen and so on. These items, and many many more, have been part of my surroundings for as long as I have had surroundings, and there was no time (at least no time worth considering, as whatever kind of experience I had as an infant is thoroughly lost to me) where these things were manifest to me in some other way: insofar as things were manifest at all, they were manifest in terms of the referential totality, whose basic shape is still roughly the same (despite the staggering changes in technological innovations since my childhood).

Befindlichkeit has a narrower dimension as well, which Heidegger discusses under the heading of *mood*. Moods too are things we find ourselves in, and are never something we choose from some moodless standpoint. At the same time, moods colour how things show up to us: going for a walk with my dog may present itself to me as, variously, an opportunity for exercise, an occasion to explore, quality time with my pal or just something to be done with as quickly as possible, depending upon the mood I bring to the task. And my mood will not just be something that changes how I 'look at' the activity, but will affect what that activity *is*: the walk with my dog really will be an occasion to explore if I bring a mood of curiosity or inquisitiveness to the situation; it will be a tedious chore if I bring a mood of impatience to it; and so on. Heidegger thus warns against interpreting moods in an overly psychological manner, tempting though that may be to do. (We should also bear in mind that moods have a kind of trans-individual way of being manifest as well. We can talk about the mood of a gathering, a neighbourhood, even an entire cultural era, and these are things that people can find themselves caught up in rather than determining or controlling.) Moods reveal what

Heidegger calls 'thrownness', which emphasizes the ways in which Da-sein finds itself already engaged and oriented in ways over which it had no say. Though the shape of my existence is an issue for me, and so presents itself as something that is responsive to my choices and decisions, that *this* existence is *my* existence to deal with was not something I ever chose or decided: being David Cerbone, rather than someone else, with *this* past, *this* upbringing, *this* orientation to the world (both in general and *this* specific way here and now), is who I find myself to be. What I ultimately choose to make of it is another matter, but any such choosing will always be on the basis of thrownness and never will be such as to circumvent or do away with that thrownness altogether. Da-sein is 'thrown possibility', which nicely summarizes the first two constitutive aspects of care.

4B DA-SEIN'S DISCURSIVE STRUCTURE

Heidegger's discussion of understanding paves the way for his consideration of interpretation, since the two are intimately connected. Interpretation is always based upon understanding, and serves to develop it so as to render it more explicit: 'In interpretation understanding does not become something different, but rather itself' (BT, p. 139/148). Heidegger's point here may be illustrated if we recall the account of breakdowns from earlier in Division One (though we need to be careful not to construe all occasions for interpretation as involving breakdowns or crises). Imagine a carpenter busily hammering in his workshop. For the most part, he may be fully absorbed in his task, driving in nails just as they need to be in all the right places. His orientation toward his situation is one of understanding – things are manifest *as* hammers, nails, tasks to be done and so on – but in a thoroughly non-thematic way. Suppose, however, that somewhere along the way, he takes a bad swing and drives the nail in aslant rather than straight into the wood. At this point, his absorption is disrupted, and his attention may become more explicitly focused on his task. That is, his circumspection will zero in on the problem nail, so that it stands out against the background of his ongoing activity. He may fuss and fiddle with the nail, ponder whether to pull it out or try to correct his earlier mistake by tapping it into a straighter position. All of this fussing, fiddling, pondering and correcting falls under the rubric of what Heidegger means by 'interpretation'. In interpretation:

What is at hand comes *explicitly* before sight that understands. All preparing, arranging, setting right, improving, rounding out, occur in such a way that things at hand for circumspection are interpreted in their in-order-to and are taken care of according to the interpretedness which has become visible. (BT, p. 139/148–9)

Interpretation thus makes explicit what was already implicitly present in understanding. Interpretation is not a matter of throwing 'a "significance" over what is nakedly objectively present' (BT, p. 140/150), but rather of more clearly delineating what was already replete with significance by virtue of its place in the referential totality. Heidegger's inclusion of such activities as 'preparing, arranging, setting right' and so on make clear that interpretation is not exclusively, or even primarily, a linguistic activity. This does not mean that interpretation cannot be linguistic, but Heidegger argues that any such linguistically articulated modes of interpretation are based or founded upon something more basic.

Statements or *assertions* are a 'derivative mode of interpretation', since an assertion puts into words what was already delineated by an interpretative regard. (A translational note: Macquarrie and Robinson translate *Aussage* as 'assertion', while Stambaugh uses 'statement'. I will use the two interchangeably.) If the carpenter were to turn to his apprentice and say, 'See? I bent the nail', or simply, 'The nail is bent', such an assertion would convey to the apprentice what the carpenter had already noticed. That assertion is a 'derivative phenomenon' does not mean that the practice of making assertions is doomed only to put into words what has already been accomplished in less fully linguistic modes of interpretation. As the example of the carpenter and the apprentice shows, a linguistic assertion facilitates communication: what gets delineated in an interpretative encounter can be more easily passed along via a linguistic assertion than by most other means. (Of course, other means of conveyance are possible: we can imagine the carpenter simply giving his apprentice a look or pointing with his finger or the end of the hammer to the bent nail.) Assertions can be easily repeated in a way that gestures, meaningful looks and emphasized actions cannot. (It is not surprising, then, that Heidegger's discussion of idle talk closely follows that of assertion.) Assertion facilitates another mode of Da-sein's comportment toward entities, however. We have already seen that interpretation narrows one's focus, so as to more explicitly delineate some particular moment of the 'in-order-to'. With assertion, that narrowing may change over to a more complete detachment. What I mean here is that by becoming the subject of an assertion, what was previously encountered as useful things (and perhaps as unhandy) can be encountered as something objectively present, as an object-with-properties. Asserting can thus effect a kind of detachment of the subject of the assertion from the context of activity in which it was initially located. If I begin an assertion with, 'The hammer . . .', then that narrows our attention entirely to the hammer, to what is going on with *it*, and so the hammer gets picked out precisely as an 'it' with its own properties or features. This need not be case, i.e. not all assertions reveal what there is as objectively present, but objective presence is the 'specialty' of assertion.

Heidegger's discussions of understanding, interpretation and assertion further emphasize the ways in which the everyday world is structurally complex, constituted and pervaded by a network of referential relations. The structural delineations of the everyday world indicate the fundamental status of what Heidegger calls 'discourse', a translation of the German, '*Rede*'. Though 'discourse', like '*Rede*', sounds like a primarily linguistic notion, Heidegger wants the term to indicate something more basic that serves to ground what is straightforwardly linguistic. That is, discourse is bound up with the way the everyday world is already carved up via relations of *significance*. The everyday world is already *articulated*, in the way that a skeleton has an articulated structure, and this kind of articulation serves as the basis for linguistic articulations in the vocal or verbal sense. 'Words accrue to significations' (BT, p. 151/162), which signals the secondary, ontical status of verbal languages in relation to the ontological category of discourse. As previous commentators have pointed out, we can get a grip on Heidegger's distinction between discourse and language proper by reminding ourselves of the different senses of 'telling'. In one sense, 'telling' is fully linguistic, as when I tell you something, which you then tell to someone else, but there are also senses that need not be linguistic, as in telling the difference between one thing and another. Discourse as Heidegger is using it here is bound up with this non-linguistic sense of telling.

To say that Da-sein is discursive is to say that Da-sein, in engaging with the world understandingly, can engage that world in a telling manner, i.e. by telling the difference between this item of equipment and that, this task and that, what this person is doing and where that person lives and so on. Rather than being confined to our explicitly linguistic capacities, such ways of telling pervade our perceptual experience generally: ' "Initially" we never hear noises and complexes of sound, but the creaking wagon, the motorcycle. We hear the column on the march, the north wind, the woodpecker tapping, the crackling fire' (BT, p. 153/163). Heidegger notes that 'it requires a very artificial and complicated attitude in order to "hear" a "pure noise" ' (BT, p. 153/164). Without these practical and perceptual sorts of tellings, there would be nothing for Da-sein to tell in the linguistic sense. This raises the question of whether there can be Da-sein without language. Heidegger is not entirely clear on this point, and scholars disagree about his stance on such a possibility. Heidegger clearly wants to indicate an ontological structure that is not simply co-extensive with the structure of any *particular* language. That would be a conflation of the ontical and the ontological. At the same time, Heidegger says that 'the way in which discourse gets expressed is language' (BT, p. 151). Given this last remark, I find it difficult to imagine such a discursive structure without the possibility of *any* ontical expression. When we consider the topic of language further on, in the context of Heidegger's later philosophy, we will see that he is far less ambiguous about the place of language. In the later philosophy, the notion of a being who has an understanding of being, who can stand in a relation to being (both of beings and as such), and yet lacks a language is a non-starter.

4C FALLING (PREY)

We still need to consider the third constitutive aspect of the care-structure – being-together-with (innerworldly beings encountered) – which Heidegger refers to as *falling*. (Stambaugh translates the German (*das Verfallen*) as 'falling prey', which I find too exclusively dark; as I discuss below, there is such a 'dark side' to Heidegger's explication of this concept, but it would be a mistake to treat this aspect as more than just one side. As with *das Man* and idle talk, Heidegger moves far too seamlessly between positive (or at least neutral) and negative characterizations of these constitutive aspects of Da-sein's existence.) Falling names my current absorption: the tasks I am currently caught up in, the projects I am undertaking and so on. Heidegger's placement of falling at the end of his formulation is meant to signal that my current absorption cannot be rendered intelligible as a free-standing time-slice (the same is true for the other two aspects as well, but Heidegger is especially concerned to stress this point in the case of falling, owing to the dominance of notions like presence and actuality in the philosophical tradition). To make sense of what I am doing *now*, one would have to appeal both to what I have been doing and where I am heading. Thus, my activity right now of sitting at a computer typing away is only the activity that it is (writing a book on Heidegger), given my already-determined situation (including, for example, my training in philosophy, my years as a professor, signing a contract to write this book and so on), and given what the typing is for, namely that it is *towards* the writing of book, which in turn is done for-the-sake-of my self-understanding as a professor of philosophy. We saw before that Husserl, in his phenomenology of perceptual experience, pointed to the horizonal character of even the simple experience of looking at a single object: what I currently see goes beyond what is visually available here and now, since that visual availability is informed by and points to moments of experience that are temporally beyond it, for example the hidden sides of the object that I have experienced, will experience or could experience were I to orient myself differently toward the object. Heidegger's point here is that human activity more generally has this kind of horizonal structure, where my current situation is informed and sustained by its relations to my past and future.

Heidegger's discussion of falling is more fraught than his treatment of *Befindlichkeit* and understanding. (This is signalled textually by its belated appearance in Chapter V, after his discussions of interpretation, understanding, discourse, and language. By the time Heidegger introduces falling, he has already located three equiprimordial aspects of being-in – *Befindlichkeit*, understanding and discourse – and so it is not entirely clear just where falling fits.) While Heidegger emphasizes that falling is as much a constitutive aspect of Da-sein's way of being as the other two, falling, as the term itself suggests, is more directly connected to Da-sein's *inauthenticity*, i.e. to Da-sein's failing to be anything other than a *Man*-self. We saw before how some phenomena have for Heidegger both a positive and negative dimension: this is especially evident in his discussion of *das Man*, which is ineliminable from the very idea of there being an intelligible world but which exerts a kind of dictatorial force in the formation and sustaining of our sensibilities. Falling is likewise both positive and negative. It is positive in the sense that I could not be projecting any possibility if there were not something I was currently doing. That is, I could not be acting for-the-sake-of some possible way to be if I were not *acting*. At the same time, falling, as naming Da-sein's *absorption* in its present situation, can also serve to distract from the task of confronting its own being as an issue. Recall the linkage for Heidegger between absorption and dispersion: as absorbed in what it is doing, Da-sein is thereby dispersed, its attention scattered in various directions. In falling, there is the risk of the world becoming an arena of *distraction*, wherein we become absorbed in what surrounds us as more of a spectacle, rather than an arena for active participation. Think here of the kind of absorption occasioned by watching television, where both past and future seem to fall away. In this mode of absorption, existence dwindles down to a quest for stimulation, for entertainment without any point or purpose beyond being entertained. Though Heidegger could not have appealed to this example, the activity of 'channel-surfing' – continuously clicking the remote control, taking in fragments of this and that show, concentrating on nothing save the change in the presently available images and sounds – might well be the paradigm case of falling in the more pejorative sense. Heidegger connects with falling the notion of idle talk, which we have already considered, but also curiosity and ambiguity, which name the pull of *novelty* without any depth of meaning. Again, in the case of channel surfing, the activity is directed by the search only for a new image, something else to watch, though without any deeper point or purpose (indeed, in channel-surfing, one does not even get as far as watching an entire television show, a potentially whole story or narrative).

It should be evident by now that the three constitutive aspects of Da-sein's way of being as care cannot be spelled out without invoking *temporal* notions. Each aspect is clearly keyed to one temporal dimension, such that understanding corresponds to the future, *Befindlichkeit* to the past and falling to the present. Though there are these clear temporal connotations, we should not understand these aspects of Da-sein's way of being as pointing to literally past, present and future moments of its existence. All of these aspects are *always* operative in Da-sein's ongoing existence. My history is not merely a set of past events and experiences, but something that currently informs what I do, how I do it and why I do it, and my possibilities do not lie off in an as yet unrealized future, but are instead what determine what I am doing here and now. Though Heidegger will argue eventually that Da-sein's way of being has a temporal structure, we need to be careful not to understand Da-sein's temporality in the way we ordinarily understand time. Indeed, how we ordinarily understand time is something Heidegger finds philosophically problematic, bound up as it is with the dominance in philosophy of the temporal present as precisely what is 'most real'. The peculiarity of Da-sein's temporal structure is further indicated by the ordering of the constitutive aspects of care in Heidegger's formulation, since read left to right we get future-past-present. In the case of Da-sein's temporality, the future precedes the past, which in turn precedes the present. The peculiarity of this ordering indicates that insofar as Da-sein is ultimately to be understood as a kind of temporal structure, its temporality cannot be understood in terms of the ordinary, clock sense of time.

CHAPTER 5

PHILOSOPHICAL IMPLICATIONS: KNOWLEDGE, REALITY AND TRUTH

The closing chapter of Division One of *Being and Time* is, like the one preceding it, a bit of a motley assortment of topics and arguments, as though Heidegger were running through a checklist of items that needed to be addressed before Division Two could commence. We have already discussed one of these, the care-structure, since Heidegger's elaboration of that structure serves to summarize and complete the discussion of being-in from the preceding chapter. Chapter VI also contains an important discussion of *Angst* or *anxiety* (Stambaugh leaves the term untranslated, but I will follow Macquarrie and Robinson here) as a 'fundamental attunement'. I will, however, postpone consideration of anxiety, as it is best discussed in conjunction with the (possible) transition from everydayness to authenticity, a central topic of Division Two. That leaves Heidegger's eminently dispensable discussion of a Latin poem that is meant to provide 'confirmation of the existential interpretation of Da-sein as care' (BT, p. 183/196), and, far less dispensable, a consideration of two weighty philosophical topics: reality and truth. We might read these latter discussions as detailing the philosophical dividends the phenomenology of everydayness pays, even prior to considering the transition from inauthenticity to authenticity.

5A KNOWLEDGE AND SCEPTICISM

Even without considering the possibility of Da-sein's authenticity explicitly, Heidegger's phenomenology can be seen already to be philosophically significant or revelatory. We have already had a glimmer of this in his treatment of the notion of world, since Heidegger thinks that one of the principal shortcomings of the

Western philosophical tradition is its tendency to pass over the phenomenon of world, thereby casting about for renderings of human existence, reality and their interrelation in phenomenologically inadequate, indeed distorted, terms. One prominent example of this kind of distortion is philosophy's preoccupation, at least since the time of Descartes, with *scepticism*. That is, philosophy since Descartes has seen as one of its primary tasks to be articulating and overcoming the sceptical predicament, wherein the human subject finds itself threatened with the possibility of radical isolation with respect to the goings-on in the world. The challenge is one of showing that this possibility does not obtain, and so that the human subject is indeed in 'contact' with, or has 'access' to, the world after all. In other words, the goal is to establish the possibility of knowledge in the face of a series of considerations that seem to lead to its impossibility.

Heidegger's response to scepticism is less than straightforward, and deliberately so, since he sees the tradition's preoccupation with epistemology to be symptomatic of deeper philosophical confusions. Thus, he does not wish to engage the tradition's epistemological problems directly, in order to provide answers to the questions it raises; rather, his main aim is to show there to be something defective about the questions themselves, and so something amiss in our urge to raise them and demand answers to them. This kind of reorientation with respect to sceptical puzzles and problems can be discerned in his rejoinder to Kant's famous 'scandal of philosophy'. What Kant considered scandalous is that no one had as yet provided a proof of the existence of 'things outside of us' in a manner that would do away with scepticism once and for all. As Heidegger sees it: 'The "scandal of philosophy" does not consist in the fact that this proof is still lacking up to now, but *in the fact that such proofs are expected and attempted again and again*' (BT, p. 190/205). Rather than provide the proof Kant had longed for, Heidegger instead wants to undermine the cogency of the demand. Considerable care is needed, however, in order to sustain this kind of response to scepticism, since at several junctures, it sounds at least like Heidegger is providing what the sceptic wanted, namely, a kind of proof of the reality of the world.

In order to get a grip on Heidegger's response to scepticism, it may help to consider first a response that is offered as far more straightforward, in the sense that it takes Kant's 'scandal of philosophy' seriously and attempts to bring the scandal to a close by supplying the needed proof. I have in mind here G. E. Moore's famous essay from 1939, 'Proof of an External World'. Moore's proof is surprisingly simple, requiring only two premises and no further intermediate steps prior to the conclusion: to prove 'the existence of things outside of us', Moore simply displays the first two 'things' he happens upon, in this case his two hands. The premises of the argument are thus the assertion, by Moore, of the existence of each of his own hands, i.e. 'Here is one hand', and 'Here is another', accompanied by the appropriate gestures. These assertions are sufficient to prove what Moore sees as needing proof.

The opening chapters of Division I of *Being and Time* might be understood as confronting Kant's scandal in a roughly Moore-like fashion. As we have seen, Heidegger insists that a proper understanding of what it is to be a human being must *begin* from the standpoint of what he calls Da-sein's 'everydayness', where that means our day-to-day, pre-theoretical mode of activity. As we have further seen, Heidegger's characterizations of that activity are replete with descriptions of Da-sein's engagement with various *entities*, namely what Da-sein encounters as things of use. Equipment consists of 'the beings encountered nearest to us' (*BT*, p. 62/66), and our encounter with, and skilful handling of, such entities marks the way 'everyday Da-sein always already *is*' (BT, p. 63/67). Although Heidegger refers to what we encounter as useful *things*, he insists that a proper understanding of them reveals that these 'things' cannot be taken as isolated material objects. Again, what it is to be any particular useful thing or item of equipment cannot be spelled out without reference to other such items: what it is to be a hammer, for instance, requires reference to other useful things, such as nails, lumber and saws. That is why Heidegger says that 'strictly speaking, there "is" no such thing as *a* useful thing'. Despite Heidegger's underscoring of the ways in which the entities we encounter and manipulate in our day-to-day lives differ from mere things, for all that, they would nonetheless appear to count as 'things to be met with in space' in Moore's sense of the term. Things like hammers and nails are not 'internal' like thoughts, nor are they like 'things' such as after-images, which *appear* as though in space, but cannot be met there. In other words, useful things have the requisite features to make them appropriate starting points for a proof like Moore's. In response to the demand for proof, that is, Heidegger's phenomenology of everydayness appears to provide a seemingly unlimited stock of Moore-type sentences to use as premises for such a 'proof'. The phenomenology of every-dayness would thus appear to provide the kind of proof Kant had demanded, and so we can use it to bring the 'scandal of philosophy' to a close.

Were Heidegger responding to the demand for proof in the same manner as Moore does, then he would be vulnerable to the same objections Moore's would-be proof faces. That is, we are apt to feel that Moore's proof comes too late, in the sense that if one has, through a process of sceptical reasoning, found reasons to call the existence of the world into question, then those reasons suffice to call into question the premises of the argument Moore con-structs. Moore is entitled to the premises of his argument only to the extent to which the existence of the external world has already been established: one needs, that is, to have secured the *conclusion* of the argument before one can be entitled to assert the premises. Despite the Moore-like tone of some of Heidegger's remarks, that he explicitly rejects the demand for proof shows a sensitivity to the question-begging character such remarks would have were they construed as sufficient to satisfy such a demand. In starting with Da-sein's everydayness, Heidegger should not be read as trying to meet sceptical demands for proof in the manner of Moore. Rather, the phenomenology of everydayness marks the beginning of a more radical reorientation toward sceptical questions and prob-lems, so that we ultimately no longer find them compelling or compulsory.

To develop this point more fully, we need to circle back to § 13 in Chapter II of Division One, where Heidegger argues that knowledge is a 'founded mode of being-in-the-world'. To say that knowledge is 'founded' is to say that knowledge depends upon some more basic mode of engagement, namely the kind of circumspective concern characteristic of Da-sein's everyday activity. The idea that know-ledge is founded on Da-sein's being-in-the-world undercuts the primacy of the appeal to the notions of 'inner' and 'outer' in terms of which the sceptical problem of knowledge is framed. The appeal to being-in-the-world effects a reorientation in how one under-stands both such notions, such that it can be said with equal legitim-acy that Da-sein is always *both* inside and outside with respect to the world:

> In directing itself toward . . . and in grasping something, Da-sein does not first go outside of the inner sphere in which it is initially encapsulated, but, rather, in its primary kind of being, it is always already 'outside' together with some being encountered in the world already discovered. Nor is any inner sphere abandoned when Da-sein dwells together with a being to be known and determines its character. Rather, even in this 'being outside' together with its object, Da-sein is 'inside,' correctly understood; that is, it itself exists as the being-in-the-world which knows. (BT, p. 58/62)

Undercut as well is thus the kind of demand for proof that is part and parcel of the traditional conception, since any question of how something in a 'subject's' 'inner sphere' relates to something 'outer' requires some antecedent justification for raising the question of knowledge in those terms. Without that justification, just *why* we should take such questions seriously becomes more difficult to make out. Indeed, with the appeal to being-in-the-world as that upon which knowledge is 'founded', that kind of explanatory project is, as Heidegger puts it, 'annihilated' (BT, p. 57/61).

For Heidegger, then, there is no 'problem of knowledge', nor is there any 'problem of the "external world"', and so he is not in the business of providing any kind of solution or answer. The world is not something that is 'presupposed' in order for knowledge to be possible, nor is it something that we have some kind of basic 'faith' in as a precondition for our judgments and activity:

> *Faith* in the reality of the 'external world,' whether justified or not, *proves* this reality for it, whether sufficiently or insufficiently, *it presupposes* it, whether explicitly or not, such attempts that have not mastered their own ground with complete transparency, presuppose a subject which is initially *worldless*, or not certain of its world, and which basically must first make certain of a world. (BT, p. 191/206)

5B TRUTH: DISCOVERY AND DISCLOSEDNESS

As Heidegger himself acknowledges, his discussion of the notion of *truth* may appear considerably belated, since 'from time immemorial, philosophy has associated truth with being' (BT, p. 196/212). If we consider an inquiry into the meaning of being as an inquiry into what beings most fundamentally *are*, that would seem already to invoke, albeit implicitly, the notion of truth: to say what beings most fundamentally are *is* to say what is most fundamentally *true* of or about them. (Such a connection is reinforced by Heidegger's conception of phenomenology as letting 'that which shows itself be seen from itself in the very way in which it shows itself from itself'. Heidegger's inclusion of 'the very way' in this formulation implies a kind of accuracy, correctness, or validity of the showing, i.e. that the way in which something shows itself is not *false*.) Thus, Heidegger notes that 'because being actually "goes together" with truth, the phenomenon of truth has already been one of the themes of our earlier analysis, although not explicitly under this name' (BT, p. 197/213). At the very conclusion of Division One, Heidegger declares that 'now we must explicitly delimit the phenomenon of truth giving precision to the problem of being and fixing the problems contained therein' (BT, p. 197/213-4). The final sections of Division One aim to do just that.

As with his treatment of knowledge, scepticism and reality, Heidegger approaches the phenomenon of truth with a critical eye cast toward traditional conceptions of it. In this case, however, he is far less wholesale in his repudiation of the tradition; rather, his concern is to reveal the traditional account's incompleteness. There is, however, an important critical move that Heidegger makes at the outset, which marks a point of commonality with his rejection of the subject–object, inner–outer model of knowledge that fuels traditional epistemological problems and puzzles. Just as Heidegger rejects a conception of knowledge as an 'inner' possession of the knowing 'subject', so too is he suspicious of the appeal to *judgement* as the primary locus or vehicle of truth. The problem with fixating on judgement is that the *act* of judging is, on the face of it, a wholly psychological notion. But the connection between truth and judgement cannot be a matter of truth's being anchored in particular psychological episodes, as that would threaten to make truth an entirely *subjective* notion, whereas the whole point of the notion of truth is to secure a notion of *objectivity*. We thus need to distinguish between the *act* of judging, which is a particular psychological process or episode, and the *content* of the judgement, which is taken to be *ideal*. Making this distinction allows us to consider what is judged as true irrespective of the particulars of any psychological episode.

Moreover, making this distinction allows us to make sense of the idea that two or more people judge the same thing to be true. If we distinguish between acts and content, this can be so even though each person has his or her own psychological processes or episodes.

Though this manoeuvre sounds promising in terms of rescuing the notions of judgement and truth from the grip of psychologism, it brings with it a host of further problems that Heidegger considers to be intractable. In particular, the problem is one of conceiving in a satisfactory manner the *relations* the various items or episodes so distinguished stand in to one another. That is, given the act–content distinction, we have to understand how it is that the act, which is a particular psychological episode or process, hooks up with a content, which is ideal, as well as how this ideal content hooks up with some real state of affairs, some goings-on in the world. Given how different in kind each of the three things to be related is, it is not at all clear how to conceive of the relations they may stand in to one another. Are the relations themselves real or ideal? If they are real, how can they hook on to something ideal? If ideal, how can they relate to something real? If the relations are neither real nor ideal, how can they relate to either domain? To break loose of these vexing problems, Heidegger proposes instead the examination of the 'phenomenal connection of demonstration', where 'the relationship of agreement must become visible' (BT, p. 200/217). That is, Heidegger suggests that we consider situations where the truth or correctness is demonstrated, so as to get clear about just *what* gets demonstrated as true and, more importantly, what *being demonstrated to be true* means or involves. The promise of this strategy is that in such a 'phenomenal connection', none of the ontologically murky items will make an appearance, and so no ontologically even murkier relations will have to be accounted for.

Heidegger's example is almost disarmingly straightforward. He asks us to imagine someone whose back is turned to the wall saying, 'The picture on the wall is askew'. Notice first that the example involves an *assertion*, an overt *statement*, which removes the aura of interiority that clung to the psychological act of judgement. The assertion, unlike the act of judgement, is something out there, open to view, and easily shared among two or more interlocutors. Indeed, the aim of making an assertion is typically to point out something to someone else. Finally, beginning with the notion of assertion would appear to avoid the dangers of psychologism noted above, as it usually seems quite easy to determine in practice whether you and I have made the same assertion or not. To turn now to the issue of *demonstration*, we may imagine this to happen when the one who made the assertion then turns towards the wall and ascertains that the picture on the wall is indeed askew. Heidegger then asks, 'What is proved in this demonstration? What is the meaning of confirming this statement [assertion]?' (BT, p. 200/217). It seems obvious to say here that what gets demonstrated is that things really are as the assertion declares; what is confirmed when the speaker turns towards the wall is that his assertion *agrees* with how things are with the picture on the wall. Heidegger wants to insist here that we not take these obvious observations and distort them by slipping in some further items. In particular, he wants to avoid any addition of some kind of mental items, artefacts of a 'psychical process', which are to serve as the real locus of agreement with how things are with the picture on the wall. No such 'representations' are involved here. In making the assertion, the speaker is directed towards the picture on the wall, even without looking, not towards a representation of the picture; when he turns towards the wall, he is even more directly in touch with the wall, but not so as to compare what he now sees with a representation had beforehand.

'Making statements [assertions] is a being toward the existing thing itself' (BT, p. 201/218), which means, first, that no further intermediaries need be invoked to explain or account for how an assertion is directed towards 'the thing itself', and, second, that the 'way of being towards' of the assertion is what Heidegger calls 'being-uncovering'. The aim of the assertion is to reveal, point out or uncover how things are with respect to some entity, entities or situation. Heidegger's appeal to 'uncovering' allows for a formulation of what it means for an assertion to be *true*: 'To say that a statement [assertion] is *true* means that it discovers the beings in themselves' (BT, p. 201/218). Notice again the congruence of this formulation with Heidegger's conception of phenomenology, which indicates that he is here discharging a debt incurred more or less at the outset of *Being and Time*.

In offering an account of the truth of assertions as being-uncovering, Heidegger takes himself to be working out ideas about truth already in play in the philosophical tradition (minus a great deal of the baggage of 'representations', 'psychic processes' and the 'subject–object' relation). Heidegger claims that in offering an account of assertoric truth as being-uncovering, he is returning to the '*oldest* tradition of ancient philosophy', which already has an understanding of truth of just this sort, albeit in 'a pre-phenomenological way' (BT, p. 202/219). Indeed, even without delving into Heraclitus and Aristotle, there seems to be something unobjectionable, even unsurprising, about saying that an assertion, when true, points out or reveals how things are with respect to the entities to which it points. The assertion, 'My coffee cup is empty', is true just when it is said on those occasions where my cup really is empty, and so where my making the assertion points out to the listener (which could even be me, if I'm talking to myself) that the cup is empty, i.e. when the assertion uncovers the cup *as* empty. However, Heidegger does not wish merely to recapitulate the philosophical tradition, even if that includes offering a more enlightened formulation of its 'pre-phenomenological' ideas. Rather, he wishes to go further in showing the *derivative* character of this traditional conception, and so articulating something of tremendous philosophical importance that the tradition has missed. This is signalled in the paragraph marking the transition from his discussion of the truth of assertions to the argument that this notion of truth is itself derived from something more basic; in that paragraph, he writes:

Being-true as discovering is in turn ontologically possible only on the basis of being-in-the-world. This phenomenon, in which we recognize a basic constitution of Dasein, is the *foundation* of the primordial phenomenon of truth. (BT, p. 201/219)

In what way is being-in-the-world 'foundational' for the assertoric truth in the sense of being-uncovering? The basic idea is this: in order for assertions to point out or uncover how entities are in various respects ('The picture on the wall is askew', 'My coffee cup is empty' and so on), entities must more generally be available or open to view. In order to point out how things are with the picture or with the cup, entities likes cups and pictures must already be manifest and understood. Heidegger can be seen here to be applying the lessons of his discussion of the relations among understanding, interpretation and assertion, where each is derived from the previous, but he is also reaching further back into Division One, to a distinction we have not thus far discussed. The distinction, which first appears in Chapter III of Division One, is between what Heidegger calls 'disclosedness' and 'discovery'. The latter is akin to the notion of uncovering we have lately been considering, as both concern the revelation of particular aspects or features of a particular entity or entities. Discovery and uncovering are thus both *ontical* notions, and so the formulation of assertoric truth Heidegger offers is a formulation of ontical truth. Heidegger introduces the notion of disclosedness as follows: ' "To disclose" and "disclosedness" are used as technical terms . . . and mean "to unlock" – "to be open" ' (BT, p. 70/75). Disclosedness is an *ontological* notion, pertaining to the ways in which beings have been 'laid open' in their being. Disclosedness thus pertains to the understanding of being, and so being-in-the-world. Indeed, Heidegger at one point declares emphatically that '*Da-sein is its disclosure*' (BT, p. 125/133), which means that Da-sein is the being to whom beings are manifest in their being, or, again, that Da-sein has an understanding of the being of entities. Disclosedness provides the foundation for discovery in the sense that Da-sein's prior openness to beings, i.e. that beings have already 'been laid open', allows for the possibility of particular discoveries or uncoverings with respect to how things are with the beings so laid open.

Disclosedness thus turns out to be 'the most primordial phenomenon of truth', that serves as the 'existential and ontological foundations of uncovering' (BT, p. 203/220). These foundations are entirely bound up with Da-sein's way of being: 'In that Da-sein essentially *is* its disclosedness, and, as disclosed, discloses and discovers, it is essentially "true." Da-sein *is* "*in the truth*" ' (BT, p. 203/221). At the same time, Heidegger warns that we must bear in mind Da-sein's *falling*, and so that Da-sein's way of being at the same time allows for entities to be closed off, misunderstood or misrepresented (this is especially the case when it comes to Da-sein's understanding of itself): 'Being closed off and covered over belong to the *facticity* of Da-sein. The full existential and ontological meaning of the statement "Dasein is in the truth" also says equiprimordially that "Dasein is in untruth" ' (BT, p. 204/222). Nonetheless, truth-as-disclosedness is still somehow more basic, since 'only in so far as Dasein is disclosed, is it also closed off' (BT, p. 204/222).

5C SELF-OWNERSHIP AND SELF-REALIZATION:
THE ROAD TO AUTHENTICITY

As the discussions of scepticism and truth make clear, Heidegger sees the phenomenology of everydayness developed in Division One as already paying philosophical dividends. This is so especially with the project he refers to back in the second Introduction of 'destructuring the history of ontology' (BT, p. 17/19). Heidegger's arguments concerning knowledge as a 'founded mode' of being-in-the-world, his displacement of the primacy of actuality or presence, his critique of the subject–object distinction, his assertion of the 'ontological priority' of useful things over what is objectively present, his diagnosis and dismissal of sceptical problems and puzzles and his two-tiered conception of truth are all offered as a sustained critique of the Western philosophical tradition. They are all illustrative of the ways in which that tradition has tended to neglect, distort or misunderstand the question of being by offering interpretations of what it means to be that both begin and end in the wrong place. Such interpretations begin, Heidegger contends, by simply 'passing over' the phenomenon of world, and so failing to apprehend and appreciate the distinctive character of Da-sein's manner of existence; as a result, these interpretations end up according pride of place to such notions as substance, theory and knowledge, and do so in ways that misconceive our relation to the world (as, for example, that of detached spectator).

Given this kind of philosophical pay-off, one is apt to feel that Heidegger's work is more or less done at the close of Division One. His explication of Da-sein's everyday existence, culminating in the elaboration of the care-structure, along with the philosophical morals to be gleaned from that explication, would appear to constitute a kind of complete philosophical account. However, Heidegger insists that his work is by no means done, and for more than one reason. First, the entire project of *Being and Time* is devoted to answering the question of the meaning of being *in general*: no matter how complete his account of Da-sein is at the end of Division One, little has been provided by way of providing an answer to that guiding question. Second, even if we leave aside his ultimate ontological aspirations, Heidegger wants to insist that even his narrower, more preliminary project of explicating the being of Da-sein is itself still radically incomplete. The incompleteness is owing to

Heidegger's neglecting thus far to elaborate on a distinction he has alluded to from early on, namely, the distinction between *authenticity* and *inauthenticity*. As a phenomenology of everydayness, Division One is primarily an account of inauthentic Da-sein (though Heidegger sometimes writes of everyday Da-sein as 'undifferentiated'). His characterization of everyday Da-sein as inauthentic accords with his broader descriptions of everyday Da-sein as 'dispersed' into *das Man*, and so as *falling* into 'idle talk' and 'distantiality'. The terms 'authentic' and 'inauthentic' translate *'eigentlich'* and *'uneigentlich'* respectively, where the stem *'eigen'* registers a sense of ownness or ownership. Thus, we should not here the terms 'authentic' and 'inauthentic' as signalling that inauthentic Da-sein is somehow not really Da-sein, as though it were counterfeit or some such thing. Everyday, inauthentic Da-sein is every bit as much Da-sein as authentic Da-sein (if it were not, the possibility of becoming authentic would be unintelligible). Inauthenticity does register a kind of failure, though, in the sense that inauthentic Da-sein fails fully to be itself, to *own* up to the kind of being that it is and live accordingly. Inauthentic Da-sein does not 'own itself', since its life is scattered this way and that in accordance with the dictates of *das Man*.

CHAPTER 6

DEATH AS THE 'END' OF DA-SEIN

Everyday Da-sein, though still Da-sein, does leave something out of account: in everydayness, Da-sein does not (yet) have itself fully in view. Hence the incompleteness Heidegger complains of at the close of Division One, which ends with a trio of questions that set the stage for Division Two:

> But *is* the most primordial, existential, and ontological constitution of Da-sein disclosed with the phenomenon of care? Does the structural manifoldness in the phenomenon of care give the most primordial totality of the being of factical Da-sein? Has the inquiry up to now gotten Da-sein *as a whole* in view at all? (BT, p. 211/230)

The last of these questions in particular points the way for the opening chapters of Division Two, though the indicated route is far from straightforward or direct. This is so because the sense of the phrase, 'as a whole', is not at all obvious, when applied to Da-sein. What kind of a 'view' is Heidegger hankering after here? Given the work of the phenomenology of everydayness in Division One, what exactly have we failed to see? The peculiarity of the phrase 'as a whole' in relation to Da-sein is (at least) twofold: first, as we have seen, 'the "essence" of Da-sein lies in its existence' (BT, p. 40/42), and so Da-sein is never to be understood in thing-like terms. As a result, wholeness cannot be understood in more or less spatial terms, so that we might have Da-sein before us, so to speak, all at once. Heidegger himself acknowledges this difficulty with the idea of Da-sein 'as a whole' when he writes:

And if existence determines the being of Da-sein and if its essence is also constituted by potentiality-of-being, then, as long as Da-sein exists, it must always, as such a potentiality, *not yet be* something? A being whose essence is made up of existence essentially resists the possibility of being comprehended as a total being. (BT, p. 215/233)

Since there is something essentially incomplete about Da-sein so long as it is, no complete view would appear to be possible.

Although Da-sein is incomplete so long as it is, it is only for so long, which suggests a different way of understanding the idea of Da-sein as a whole: when Da-sein has reached its *end*, when it no longer is at all, its existence is thereby bounded and so, in that sense, whole. Da-sein has run its course 'from its "beginning" to its "end"' (BT, p. 215/233), and it would appear that the entirety of that course can be surveyed. But herein lies the second peculiarity of the phrase 'as a whole' when applied to Da-sein, especially with respect to the attempt to bring that whole into view: when Da-sein has reached its end, come to completion or run its course, then it is *no longer Da-sein*, and so whatever is left to view is certainly not 'Da-sein as a whole'. Whatever 'whole' there is to grasp is certainly not Da-sein. As Heidegger notes:

However, if Da-sein 'exists' in such a way that there is absolutely nothing more outstanding for it, it has also already thus become no-longer-being-there. Eliminating what is outstanding in its being is equivalent to annihilating its being. As long as Da-sein *is* as a being, it has never attained its 'wholeness.' But if it does, this gain becomes the absolute loss of being-in-the-world. It is then never again to be experienced *as a being*. (BT, p. 220/236)

What is manifest is thus not Da-sein in this case, but perhaps only what used to be or once was Da-sein. This is a far cry from Heidegger's demand concerning the 'primordiality' of his investigations: being primordial requires making Da-sein itself manifest as a whole, and this cannot be done from a post-Da-sein vantage point.

Heidegger's worry here is especially compelling if we understand his demand that Da-sein be manifest as a whole as requiring that a particular Da-sein be manifest *to itself* as a whole. Though it is strictly speaking true that any Da-sein that has reached its end, cashed in its final 'not yet', can, as Heidegger says, 'never again be experienced *as an entity*', there is still a very definite sense in which the *whole* of that life is now surveyable, and in a way that was not possible prior to that end. Any such surveying will be necessarily retrospective or recollective, since we cannot make the episodes of the person's life literally present before us again, but to expect or demand otherwise indulges a rather bizarre fantasy and so would appear to carry little in the way of philosophical weight. But even this retrospective way of apprehending Da-sein as a whole fails when applied to the first-person case: my existence cannot be manifest to me as a whole, not just since right now *my* existence is still ongoing (that's true in the third-person case as well), but because once I have reached my 'end', there will be no longer be a 'me' to apprehend my own (now completed) existence. My end is, of course, my *death*, and that is not something I live through or experience, at least not in any way that leaves me *here*. Death marks the end of my worldly existence, which means that I am unable to apprehend that existence 'as a whole', certainly not in a manner that is of use for phenomenology: even if we allow as coherent the idea of 'postmortem phenomenology', conducted from the perspective of an 'afterlife', its results are not available for general circulation among those still living; more specifically, any such postmortem phenomenology of *my* existence as a whole is not available to me *now* (or at any time in *this* life).

6A RETHINKING DA-SEIN'S WHOLENESS

If the wholeness Heidegger is seeking rests on these sorts of requirements (bringing the life of another back into view or gaining a postmortem perspective on my own existence), then his seeking would be in vain. Indeed, as I have suggested, the demand would amount to little more than fantasy. Heidegger himself is deeply suspicious of these ways of cashing out 'as a whole', not just because of their fantastical proportions but because they are ultimately predicated on misconceptions of Da-sein's existence:

> Did we not conclude in a merely formal argumentation that it is impossible to grasp the whole of Da-sein? Or did we not at bottom inadvertently posit Da-sein as something objectively present ahead of which something not yet objectively present constantly moves along? (BT, p. 220/236–7)

The accessibility Heidegger seeks requires that 'an ontologically adequate, that is, an *existential* concept of death has been attained' (BT, p. 216/234). What Heidegger wants to obtain here is not immediately clear, especially since 'existential' and 'death' appear to pull against one another: what would an existing death be and why, moreover, might that matter for Heidegger's philosophical project?

Though there is something misleading in the worries raised about thinking through death, understood as the end of existence, in phenomenological terms, in that they may 'inadvertently' posit Da-sein as something objectively present, they nonetheless provide clues for working out what an existential conception of death might be. There is something profound in the almost trivial-sounding idea that our own deaths are not something we live through or experience; such an idea marks out death as a kind of *limit* upon each of us, a boundary on our respective capacities and potentialities. While it is often pleasing or comforting to think that everything, or at least anything, is possible, death reminds us that this is not so: our possibilities are inescapably finite. An existential conception of death may be thought of as a way of rigorously developing this finitude, of making this finitude manifest or present *within* Da-sein's existence. Rather than treat the finite, bounded character of existence as something that can only be (impossibly, fantastically) grasped from the far side of a boundary lying somewhere ahead of us in an objectively present sort of way, Heidegger's discussion of death is meant to make Da-sein's finitude phenomenologically available, to be experienced or, better, faced up to.

'Death' in Heidegger's 'existential' sense is not to be confused with 'being dead', nor with the set of events, however defined, immediately preceding and culminating in the changeover from being alive to being dead (what is often meant by 'dying'). Such events, states and transitions, along with the questions we might raise about them, are legitimate topics for such fields as biology (what is the biological definition of 'death'?), law (at what point, or under what circumstances, should someone be declared dead?) and religion (what happens to someone after death?), among others, but they are not what interest Heidegger. For Heidegger, none of these questions is properly ontological (they are instead confined to particular ontical domains), and all of them only concern death understood as a particular, discrete event (though the causes and details may vary considerably), occurring at a particular time (whenever that turns out to be). As we have seen, exclusive concern with that event, either with fixing its precise medical or legal definition or, in the individual case, wondering about when and how it might occur, does not yield much in the way of phenomenological insight: since the event is 'out there', off in the future, nothing about it is manifest to me now, and when the 'time comes', so to speak, nothing will be manifest at all. An existential conception of death, by contrast, conceives of death as a *possibility*, not in the sense of something that might occur in the way that rain tomorrow is a possibility, but, in keeping with Heidegger's technical sense of 'possibility', a way for Da-sein to project itself. But what could it mean for Da-sein to project death as a possibility? In what way could *death* be a way to live?

To sort out these questions, we first need to head off a potential confusion. One, perhaps tempting, way of answering these questions would be along the lines of the 'Live fast, die young, leave a beautiful corpse' philosophy of living, where one presumably lives in such a way as to encourage the arrival of death. One might also be tempted to think of a life that is informed by a pervasive fear of death, so that someone living in such a manner sees the possibility of death in every thing she does. Living in such a way as to hasten one's own death and living in a constant fear of death both still involve death only as an event at the terminus of a life, and so we have not yet reached death understood as a possibility in Heidegger's special sense.

Heidegger's explication of death as a possibility involves three constitutive, overlapping features or characteristics. All of these characteristics can in turn be explicated in relation to our ordinary understanding of death as an event, but they are in the end detachable from that understanding at least to the extent of pointing to something potentially more pervasive to Da-sein's existence than something that is going to happen some time or other. Rather, they are constitutive of what Heidegger calls 'being-toward-death', which is a way for Da-sein to *be*, as opposed to something that will happen *to* it. The three features are these: death is Da-sein's (1) ownmost, (2) non-relational possibility, which is (3) not to be bypassed or outstripped. Let us take these features in order, though it will become clear that they mutually inform and sustain one another.

To say that death is *ownmost* means that my death is just that: exclusively my own. While the actual event may be delayed or postponed, avoided on this occasion and deferred on that one, my death can in no way be delegated to, or appropriated by, someone else. Another person may, on some occasion, die for me, but only in the sense of *instead of* me: in doing so, that person dies his or her own death and still leaves me my death as before. Compare this to what happens when someone pays off a debt for me, or teaches a class for me or delivers a package for me: in cases like these, the other person's doing it means that I no longer have to. As Heidegger puts it, most of Da-sein's possibilities involve the possibility of represen-tation, of one Da-sein taking the place of another:

> Indubitably, the fact that one Da-sein *can be represented* by another belongs to the possibilities-of-being of being-with-one-another in the world. In the everydayness of taking care of things, constant use of such representability is made in many ways. (BT, pp. 222–3/239)

Death does not work this way:

> However, this possibility of representation gets completely stranded when it is a matter of representing the possibility of being that constitutes the coming-to-an-end of Da-sein and gives it its totality as such. *No one can take the other's dying away from him.* Someone can go 'to the death for an other.' However, that always means to sacrifice oneself for the other '*in a definite matter.*' Such dying for . . . can never, however, mean that the other has thus had his death in the least taken away. Every Da-sein must itself actually take dying upon itself. Insofar as it 'is,' death is always essentially my own. (BT, p. 223/240)

To say that death is *non-relational* means that death is a possibility Da-sein projects (or has to project), regardless of the relations it stands in to others, its tasks and its projects. Most of Da-sein's pos-sibilities *are* relational in that Da-sein's projecting them does depend on just those sorts of relations: I can only project myself as a pro-fessor insofar as there are such things as universities, academic departments, students, classrooms, course schedules and so on; I can only project myself as a husband insofar as there is the institu-tion of marriage and, of course, my wife. Projecting myself as being-toward-death does not require or depend on any such relations: I am always dying (always mortal) no matter what relations I stand in to my environing world.

The non-relational character of death gives us some insight as to why death is also *not to be bypassed* (or outstripped): that death is insensitive to the myriad relations I might stand in indicates that death has a kind of non-optional character. Possibilities that are relational can be added or deleted: I may give up being a professor or a husband, and so trade in my relational possibilities for others; moreover, those possibilities may collapse whether I like it or not (I am denied tenure, the university goes bust, my wife ups and leaves me), and so I will find myself standing in different relations to my environing world. Such changes in no way affect my mortality, which serves to underscore the special way in which death is indelibly my own. 'Death is the possibility of the absolute impossibility of Da-sein' (BT, p. 232/250). As a possibility, death always 'lies ahead' of Da-sein for Da-sein to project itself into or in terms of; as the possibility of the *impossibility* of Da-sein, death imposes a limit upon all the other possibilities Da-sein might project itself in terms, rendering each and every one of them (and so Da-sein itself) finite. Nothing I choose to do, no way in which I choose to be, can be such that I can do or be it forever; there is no way in which *all* possibilities are available to me, either simultaneously or serially. Death – not the actual event, of course, but as *'an eminent* imminence' (BT, p. 232/251) – clearly delineates *this* life precisely as my *one* life, with its irreversible history and finite allotment of *time* (however much time that turns out to be). Death thus makes vivid the idea that I *have* time, that there is a time that is 'mine' to be *used*, perhaps wisely perhaps wastefully: only a being who can acknowledge its mortality in this way can bear this sort of relation to time. As Heidegger puts it, since Da-sein is a being who 'is concerned *about its being* in its very being, then care must need "time" and thus reckon with "time"' (BT, p. 217/235).

6B DEATH AND EVERYDAYNESS

In working through the 'formal' problems above with getting Da-sein into view 'as a whole', we saw that Heidegger finds problematic both the first-personal and third-personal attempts to achieve this point of view: I cannot bring my life as a whole into view because I am still living it and when I have stopped living it, I will no longer be able to bring anything into view as I will have no view to speak of; but I also cannot bring the life of another into view as a whole, since when he has reached his end, he too is no longer there to bring into view at all. This balance between the first-person and third-person points of view is disrupted in Heidegger's less formal 'existential' conception of death. The existential conception of death is radically first-personal in nature, as it essentially involves the idea of Da-sein projecting *itself* onto, or in terms of, a possibility which is distinctively its own: my finitude or mortality, as ownmost, non-relational and not to be outstripped, is wholly mine, and while I may try to evade or deny that finitude, it can never be taken over by, or passed on to, someone else. Still, one might well wonder why a third-person perspective fails to make this kind of finitude available. After all, each of us learns early on that people *die*. We hear about the deaths of others on a more or less daily basis. Usually, these are not the deaths of anyone we know personally, but alas, this is not always the case: we do experience the deaths of friends and family members, colleagues and acquaintances, and as we grow older, these losses become more commonplace if they were not already. Do not these experiences contribute to a sense of finitude, indeed of its inevitability? It is not clear to me that they do not, but Heidegger emphasizes the pernicious tendencies of these sorts of experiences. That is, Heidegger argues, odd as this may sound, that these experiences serve by and large to allay any sense of death's being my possibility here and now. In other words, experiencing the deaths of others contributes to Da-sein's tendency to evade or cover over its own finitude. This is so primarily because the deaths of others are experienced as terminating *events*, something that happens at the end, and to end, a person's life. Such experiences contribute to a purely futural way of thinking about death, as something that will happen somewhere off in the distance, thereby encouraging the thought that 'one also dies at the end, but for now one is not involved' (BT, p. 234/253). As Heidegger notes, 'In such talk, death is understood as an indeterminate something which first has to show up from somewhere, but which right now is *not yet objectively present* for oneself, and is thus no threat' (BT, p. 234/253). In other words, 'Dying, which is essentially and irreplaceably mine, is distorted into a publicly occurring event which *das Man* encounters' (BT, p. 234/253).

Thinking of death as an objectively (someday to be) present event out there in the future leaves Da-sein with nothing to take over or project here and now, and so this way of thinking serves to hold death at arm's length (or further). Heidegger's appeals to *das Man* in these passages indicate that this evasive attitude with respect to death is part and parcel of everydayness, part of Da-sein's 'falling' whereby it is absorbed and dispersed into the anonymous norms constitutive of its day-to-day routines. 'Entangled, everyday being-toward-death is a constant *flight from death*. Being *toward* the end has the mode of *evading that end* – reinterpreting it, understanding it inauthentically, and veiling it' (BT, p. 235/254). Everydayness thus amounts to a kind of tranquillization with respect to death, an evasive fleeing that covers over death and, where it doesn't, represents death in a way that only encourages Da-sein's 'fleeing'. Death is an event that befalls others, never oneself, and insofar as death 'applies' to oneself, it is only as a distant eventuality, something that may be calculated, perhaps, via statistics, actuarial tables, medical records and so on. All such calculative thinking does not bring death any closer as *possibility*, but is instead only a way of 'thinking about this possibility, how and when it might be actualized' (BT, p. 241/261). Calculative thinking of this kind is thus not a way of living one's own death, projecting it ahead of oneself as one's 'ownmost possibility'.

Das Man, as the anonymous authority of everydayness, fosters Da-sein's tranquil attitude toward death, wherein death is either not considered at all or (mis)represented as a distant event. Here we see again what I called the 'darker side' of everydayness. In particular, we see the more pernicious tendencies of everyday 'idle talk'. We saw before that Heidegger regards idle talk as both inevitable (to speak is to be repeatable) and even positive (being able to repeat what others say is necessary to full communication), but idle talk can also exacerbate Da-sein's dispersal in everydayness. That is, idle talk cuts Da-sein off from the *sources* of the meaning of the talk. Where this is a matter of rack-and-pinion steering, microprocessors, low dispersion optics and other technical minutiae, this is to be expected and hardly ever to be reproached: no one can have a first-hand acquaintance with everything and it would be foolish to expect otherwise. The situation is far less rosy, however, when the 'source' Da-sein is cut off from is Da-sein itself, when, in other words, idle talk serves to misrepresent the nature and structure of Da-sein's own existence. *Das Man's* admittedly idle talk about death, by treating death as a distant event, soothes by making any thoughts of death easy to dismiss: these thoughts do not apply to life in the present, and so where they persist they are marks of an excessively morbid temperament or even a kind of cowardly fear. *Das Man*, Heidegger emphatically says, '*does not permit the courage to have* Angst [anxiety] *about death*' (BT, p. 235/254).

6C DEATH AND ANXIETY

Heidegger's appeal to *anxiety* here refers back to the last chapter of Division One, where he first introduces the notion. Though anxiety is discussed prior to Heidegger's treatment of questions concerning reality and truth, I have postponed considering it until now because of its role in motivating the transition from Division One to Division Two, as well as its intimate connection with the existential conception of death. Anxiety can thus be postponed no longer and must now be considered in some detail.

Heidegger refers to anxiety as a '*Grundstimmung*', a fundamental attunement or mood. As bound up with thrownness and *Befindlichkeit*, all moods are in some way disclosive or revelatory of 'being-in-the-world as a whole'. That is, whatever mood I find myself in thereby conditions or determines how *everything* shows up to me and is thereby constitutive of anything's showing up at all. What is distinctive about anxiety as a fundamental attunement or mood is that it is revelatory not just of being-in-the-world 'as a whole', but of being-in-the-world *as such*. We may understand this to mean that anxiety lays bare the structure of Da-sein's existence, stripped clean of the particularities of its daily commitments and projects. Indeed, anxiety just is the experience of disconnection from one's commitments and projects. In anxiety:

> The totality of relevance discovered within the world of things at hand and objectively present is completely without importance. It collapses. The world has the character of complete insignificance. In *Angst* we do not encounter this or that thing which, as threatening, could be relevant. (BT, p. 174/186)

That no particular thing shows up as threatening means that anxiety is to be sharply distinguished from *fear*, despite a certain qualitative similarity. In terms of how it *feels*, anxiety has all the trappings of fear, but part of what makes anxiety so unsettling is the absence of anything that is prompting these feelings or toward which such feelings are directed. (Fear, by contrast, is always directed toward something, where 'something' should be construed broadly to include situations and eventualities, as well as objects and agents: 'The only threat which can be "fearsome" and which is discovered in fear always comes from innerwordly beings' (BT, p. 174/185–6).)

From the outset of *Being and Time*, Heidegger has characterized Da-sein as a being whose being is an issue for it. Anxiety is revelatory of just that: in anxiety, Da-sein confronts its existence *as* an issue, as something not yet determined and so constituted precisely by a 'not yet'. The revelatory character of anxiety is to be distinguished from any kind of concrete deliberation, though deliberation may be the occasion for the onset of anxiety. For example, if I am growing disaffected with being a philosophy professor, I may consider other possibilities: returning to school, a career in law or business and so on. Entertaining these other possibilities, as well as the possibility of leaving the familiar environment of academia, may prompt apprehension, even fear: the other possibilities I may project myself in terms of have an air of unfamiliarity about them, and so all of them carry a sense of the unknown. These various fears may be supplanted by anxiety when I step back from entertaining this or that possibility – 'That for which *Angst* [anxiety] is anxious is not a definite kind of being and possibility of Da-sein' (BT, p. 175/188) – and instead become aware of myself simply as *confronting possibilities*, as, that is, having to choose: '*Angst* [anxiety] reveals in Da-sein its *being toward* its ownmost potentiality of being, that is, being free for the freedom of choosing and grasping itself' (BT, p. 176/188). In making manifest Da-sein's 'ownmost potentiality-for-being', anxiety thereby serves to *individualize* Da-sein:

> *Angst* [anxiety] individuates Da-sein to its ownmost being-in-the-world which, as understanding, projects itself essentially upon possibilities. Thus along with that for which it is anxious, *Angst* [anxiety] discloses Da-sein as *being-possible*, and indeed as what can be individualized in individuation of its own accord. (BT, p. 176/187–8)

Notice that Heidegger here talks of Da-sein's '*ownmost* being-in-the-world', which signals the intimate connection between anxiety and death. In confronting my existence as being-possible, I at the same time confront the possibility of the impossibility of that exist-ence. In other words, I confront my potentiality-for-being as bounded or delimited, and so as *finite*. That I cannot evade or in any way delegate my finitude delineates my existence precisely as my own: 'Anticipation lets Da-sein understand that it has to take over solely from itself the potentiality-of-being in which it is concerned absolutely about its ownmost being. Death does not just "belong" in an undifferentiated way to one's own Da-sein, but it *lays claim* on it as something *individual*' (BT, p. 243/263). Notice that Heidegger here writes of anticipation, rather than fear, since what is confronted in anxious being-toward-death is not the prospect of some particu-lar event that may or may not come to pass. Death, understood as an event, may always be eluded and so my fears in the face of such an event may be allayed, but however my fears may be quelled on some occasion, that does nothing to diminish my finitude in the least. Da-sein's possibilities 'are determined by the *end*, and so understood as *finite*' (BT, p. 244/264), which is as much as to say that Da-sein is not, and can never be, *endless*.

CHAPTER 7

GUILT AND RESOLUTENESS

As Heidegger develops the transition to authenticity in Division Two, what I have been calling the 'darker side' of everydayness becomes more prominent in his account. We have already seen how *das Man* circulates a soothing brand of idle talk about death, depicting death solely as a kind of distant event that is of no concern *now*, so that Da-sein is cut off from a proper understanding of its own finitude. Lacking insight into the nature of its own existence, remote from itself, caught up in the demands of the moment, everyday Da-sein is thereby *lost*, not by finding itself in an unfamiliar region (Da-sein's everyday environment is pervaded by familiarity) but precisely by failing to find itself at all. For Heidegger, 'finding' does not mean stumbling upon some hidden self in the way one might find a lost object by rummaging through the closet. Such a thing-like way of thinking is wholly inappropriate to Da-sein's way of being; rather, to say that Da-sein is lost means that it fails to be what it is, which in turn means that it fails to project itself. Everyday Da-sein, as Da-sein, is indeed projected, but in a manner that is largely passive:

> With the lostness in *das Man*, the nearest, factical potentiality-of-being of Da-sein has always already been decided upon – tasks, rules, standards, the urgency and scope of being-in-the-world, concerned and taking care of things. *Das Man* has always already taken the apprehension of these possibilities-of-being away from Da-sein. *Das Man* even conceals the way it has silently disburdened Da-sein of the explicit *choice* of these possibilities. (BT, pp. 247–8/268)

Heidegger's appeal here to explicit choice makes clear the character of the transition from being 'lost' in *das Man* to authenticity.

Being authentic is not so much a matter of discovering or reflecting some genuine 'inner' condition as it is taking over and projecting one's possibilities for oneself, and so living in a manner that more genuinely reflects the kind of being one is (i.e. a being that projects itself onto possibilities). Authenticity is thus a kind of return to oneself, a gathering of oneself from one's dispersal into *das Man*. The first step toward authenticity, therefore, involves the recognition of one's dispersed condition, and so a recognition that one's dispersal needs to be remedied:

> When Da-sein thus brings itself back from *das Man*, the *Man*-self is modified in an existentiel manner [i.e. a particular, ontical modification, rather than a structural, ontological one] so that it becomes *authentic* being-one's-self. This must be accomplished by *making up for not choosing*. But making up for not choosing signifies *choosing to make this choice* – deciding for a potentiality-for-being, and making this decision from one's own self. (BT, p. 248/268)

7A DA-SEIN'S INDEBTEDNESS

But how is this recognition effected? What shows to me that my usual way of getting about in the world amounts to a 'dispersal' into anonymous norms? Heidegger's accounts of anxiety and death would seem to be crucial here, since anxiety serves as an abrupt disruption of my usual routines and attitudes, while death serves to delineate for me an 'ownmost' possibility, irrespective of my place in the 'referential totality' of everydayness. For Heidegger, however, anxiety and death are not sufficient for accounting for the nature and possibility of authenticity. More is needed to facilitate the kind of recognition the transition depends upon, as well as understanding just what transition is being made. To start with the first of these, Heidegger insists that something must serve to 'attest' to Da-sein's condition, both as lost and as potentially authentic: 'But because Da-sein is *lost* in *das Man*, it must first *find* itself. In order to find *itself*, it must be "shown" to itself in its possible authenticity. In terms of its *possibility*, Da-sein *is* already a potentiality-for-being-its-self, but it needs to have this potentiality attested' (BT, p. 248/268).

Heidegger's talk of Da-sein's 'making up for not choosing' indicates another key concept beyond anxiety and death, namely *guilt*. 'Guilt' translates the German *Schuld*, which is a more multivalent word than the English translation. Though *Schuld* can mean guilt in the specifically moral or legal sense, other translations include 'debt', 'indebtedness', 'obligation', 'fault', 'cause' and 'blame', as well as 'offence' and 'sin'. Many of these senses are in play in understanding the idea that Da-sein is guilty, but we need to be especially careful to avoid misconstruing what those senses really mean here. To say that Da-sein is (always) guilty does not mean that there is some particular act or action that it has either done or failed to do, so that it can now be held responsible for that commission or omission. Nor does it mean that Da-sein has a specific debt that it can now undertake to pay off, so that, once paid, Da-sein will no longer be indebted. Heidegger is careful to ward off the nearly inevitable legalistic and moralistic understandings of *Schuld*/guilt (if Heidegger had written in English and had himself chosen the term 'guilt', he would need to be doubly careful, since it is very difficult *not* to hear 'guilt' as connoting some kind of moral or legal offence). Da-sein's *existential* guilt must be understood differently, and we can get a sense of this alternative understanding by considering further the idea that Da-sein overcomes its dispersal in *das Man* by choosing its possibilities, or, more exactly, by choosing to choose its possibilities. The revelation of Da-sein's guilt heralds this moment of choice in the form of a *call*, what Heidegger calls the 'call of conscience' (again, it is difficult to hear this without any moral connotations): 'The call of conscience has the character of *summoning* Da-sein to its ownmost potentiality-of-being-a-self, by summoning it to its ownmost quality of being a lack' (BT, p. 249/269).

Da-sein's 'ownmost being-guilty', in keeping with the multivalent meaning of *Schuld*, has more than one dimension or direction. Viewed retrospectively, Da-sein experiences itself as guilty in the sense of having to 'make up' for not having chosen before. Guilt is in this way bound up with Da-sein's thrownness insofar as Da-sein always finds itself in the midst of an ongoing project, where various aspects of that project are manifest as already settled or determined. Very roughly, I did not choose to be born, nor to be born into my particular environment, and I had very little in the way of control over the specifics of my upbringing (not to mention the specifics of my embodiment). I did not choose to be me, rather than someone else: 'Da-sein exists as thrown, brought into its there *not* of its own accord' (BT, p. 262/284). Viewed prospectively, however, Da-sein's guilt should be understood more as a sense of obligation, in that the call of conscience reveals to Da-sein its *having* to choose. Da-sein experiences itself as *burdened* with the task of choosing. This retrospective–prospective character of Da-sein's guilt is captured by Heidegger's formulation that Da-sein is revealed to itself as 'that it is and has to be', and later in his characterization of the call of conscience:

> The summons calls back by calling forth: *forth* to the possibility of taking over in existence the thrown being that it is, *back* to thrownness in order to understand it as the null ground that it has to take up into existence. (BT, p. 264/287)

The call calls Da-sein back to itself, while at the same time urging it forward (Heidegger says at one point that in the call 'lies the factor of a jolt', but quickly adds that this 'abrupt arousal' only 'reaches him who wants to be brought back' (BT, p. 251/271).

7B AUTHENTICITY AS RESOLUTENESS

Da-sein's existential guilt thus resides in the dual recognition that, as thrown, it is not the basis of its own being *and*, as projective, it is nonetheless responsible for its being: 'Da-sein is not itself the ground of its being, because the ground first arises from its own project, but as a self, it is the *being* of its ground. The ground is always ground only for a being whose being has to take over being-the-ground' (BT, p. 262/285). Of course, Da-sein may fail 'to take over being-the-ground', in that the revelations afforded by anxiety and the call of conscience may go unheeded, be misunderstood or be so unsettling as to send Da-sein fleeing back into the tranquillity of everydayness. After all, everydayness on Heidegger's account offers comforting reassurances about the perpetual postponement of death, encourages the sense of all of us being in this together and actively promotes the attitude of getting along by going along (how else *would* anything ever get done?). On the other hand, one can heed the call and thereby ignore the idle talk of *das Man*, so as to face up to the finitude of one's existence and one's ultimate responsibility for it despite not having chosen the initial conditions or even to exist at all.

Heidegger calls this latter attitude or orientation – 'the *reticent projecting oneself upon one's ownmost being-guilty which is ready for Angst* [anxiety]' (BT, p. 273/297) – *resoluteness*. Being resolute means projecting oneself in the light both of one's thrownness and one's finitude; being resolute thus means living in a way that reflects most fully the notion that one is a being whose being is an issue.

Although Heidegger's notions of anxiety, death, guilt, conscience, resoluteness and so ultimately authenticity have a highly individualistic, go-it-alone tone to them, they should not be understood as recommending or endorsing any kind of isolationism. Authentic Da-sein does not withdraw from society or forego the referential totality articulated by *das Man*: 'Even resolutions are dependent upon *das Man* and its world. Understanding this is one of the things that resolution discloses, in that resoluteness first gives to Da-sein its authentic transparency' (BT, p. 275/299). Authentic Da-sein understands this because the call of conscience has attested to its existential guilt in the sense of its inescapable indebtedness to the world in which it finds itself. Though I may disown my origins, endeavour to start afresh and so on, the ways in which I do so are still pervaded by my (largely unchosen) life until now: that I disown *this*, rather than something else, that I start anew in *this* way, that I find *these* things worth endorsing and *these* things worth rejecting, all of this is partly determined, and so revelatory of, my thrownness. Heidegger is equally clear that authenticity does not involve any kind of withdrawal from the company of others. Indeed, he suggests that it is only when one resolutely acknowledges the kind of being one is (and projects oneself accordingly) that a genuine sense of community becomes possible:

> The 'world' at hand does not become different as far as 'content,' the circle of the others is not exchanged for a new one, and yet the being toward things at hand which understands and takes care of things, and the concerned being-with with the others is now defined in terms of their ownmost potentiality-of-being-a-self. (BT, p. 274/297–8)

Authenticity is communal insofar as it makes possible genuine communication and community, freed of the trappings of conventional exchanges and rituals. As authentic, I no longer simply talk as one talks (though I don't necessarily talk differently in the sense of using a different language or even pattern of speech); rather, I speak for myself and speak with others as particular individuals, rather than as occupiers of conventionally defined social roles.

Finally, it should be emphasized that the achievement of authenticity is not a once-and-for-all matter. It would be surprising if it were, since Da-sein is not a once-and-for-all kind of entity, so long as it exists. Heidegger notes that 'Da-sein is always already in irresoluteness, and perhaps will be soon again' (BT, p. 275/299), which suggests that the kind of 'attestation' anxiety and the call of conscience afford must be experienced repeatedly. Though Da-sein may on occasion find itself, it may just as easily lose itself once again.

7C TIME AND TEMPORALITY

Even the perplexed reader may have noticed the degree to which Heidegger, in developing his phenomenology from the outset of Division One to Division Two's preoccupation with authenticity, has relied upon temporal notions. The very notion of *everydayness* (how Da-sein is everyday, as opposed to other, perhaps exceptional *times*) already suggests that understanding Da-sein involves or requires understanding its relation to time. The care-structure Heidegger explicates at the close of Division One makes this suggestion far more emphatically, as the three aspects or dimensions of care – understanding (projection), *Befindlichkeit* and falling – are temporally inflected through and through, with each aspect corresponding to one of the three temporal tenses, past, present and future. Finally, Heidegger's account of the transition to authenticity, as the resolute confrontation with one's own mortality, is likewise temporal in nature, though the existential conception of death warns us away from thinking of authentic Da-sein as preoccupied with death as some temporally distant *event*. Indeed, the peculiarities of the existential conception of death, with its sharp distinction between *anticipation* and *awaiting* (the latter is an inauthentic attitude toward death, where one wonders when 'it' is going to happen, while anticipation means embracing death as one's ownmost possibility, an ever-present way in which to project oneself), indicates that Heidegger is not simply appealing to time as something measured on the clock or haggled over by theoretical physicists. And as we have already seen, these peculiarities are even more vivid in the way Heidegger chooses to order the aspects of the care-structure, from future to past to present. Collectively, these peculiarities signal Heidegger's goal of revealing a more 'primordial' kind of time, which he refers to as *temporality*. The final chapters of Division Two begin the work of laying out this notion of temporality and its relation to time as it is ordinarily understood. Moreover, the final chapters also begin the project of showing how the different ways of *being* that have been revealed throughout the preceding chapters can themselves be understood in terms of time: time, according to Heidegger, is the 'horizon' of being, and so the key to answering the question of the meaning of being in general.

This pair of projects – mapping being onto time and deriving time from temporality – is by no means completed by the close of *Being and Time*. The final chapters of the work are compressed and frustratingly sketchy (some have suggested that Heidegger hastily finished *Being and Time* in response to professional pressures, which would explain the cobbled-together feel of the last bits of the book), and so little more than a promissory note. (This promissory note is on offer from the outset of *Being and Time*, since Heidegger had announced at the end of the second Introduction that there was to be a Division Three, as well as a second part, itself consisting of three divisions.) Recently, one commentator has argued that Heidegger's most ambitious project, the derivation of time from temporality, is a failure and, moreover, that Heidegger came to recognize it as such. As a result, he never really cashed the promissory note and instead set out in new directions in subsequent years in ways that we'll explore in Part II of this book.

PART II

HEIDEGGER'S LATER PHILOSOPHY

CHAPTER 8

NEW PATHWAYS FOR THINKING

What is often referred to as Heidegger's 'later philosophy' covers everything he wrote from the early 1930s until the end of his life some four decades later. Given the span to which this label is affixed, it is not surprising that no ready summary of Heidegger's thinking over these many years is forthcoming. Heidegger's philosophy during these years ranges over everything from works of art to the advent of technology, from the earliest Greek philosophers to Nietzsche's pivotal position in modern thought. But it is not just the breadth of Heidegger's work that makes it resistant to easy summary; rather, the resistance is in large part due to the inherent nature of his later work. What I mean here is that Heidegger pursues his philosophical concerns in a way that deliberately does not add up to one overarching theory or view. One can get a sense of this deliberate refusal to systematize by considering the title he gave to one collection of his later essays: *Holzwege*. A *Holzweg* is a timber track, a pathway used by woodcutters for accessing trees and hauling out lumber. (Another collection – *Wegmarken* or *Pathmarks* – also invokes the notion of a way or path.) A *Holzweg* thus leads one into and through the forest, to various stands of timber at various points in the forest. Since any forest consists of numerous trees, each path will likely lead in a different direction and come to a stop at a different place (on the dedication page, Heidegger describes these 'mostly overgrown' and so seldom used paths as coming 'to an abrupt stop', where what lies beyond them is 'untrodden'). Any such stopping point will unlikely be anything like a 'final destination', and so any path can always be extended further in either the same or a new direction. Even in one contiguous forest, there may be many such pathways, some of which connect with one another, some of which do not, and the pathways may be very different from one another (though Heidegger warns that they may appear to be identical, without in fact being so), depending upon whether they are being used by a single woodcutter or by a company with large trucks and other machinery.

There is little doubt that Heidegger wishes to invoke this imagery of multiple, variously connected, potentially extendable paths as characterizing his philosophical writing. His invocation of such imagery alerts us to adjust our expectations when sitting down to read his work, as we will surely go wrong if we come to it expecting to find any kind of singular philosophical theory, with a clear set of theses accompanied by a battery of arguments. Instead, Heidegger's later essays are invitations to accompany him down various pathways, to listen in on, partake of and perhaps continue his *thinking* about the topic at hand. His later writings, as ventures down different pathways, emphasize this activity of thinking far more than the enshrinement of any finished thoughts. Indeed, one of Heidegger's principal worries is that we go in all too much for such finished thoughts, for neatly encapsulated, all-encompassing views with ready answers to our questions. The rise of the natural sciences have no doubt encouraged this attitude, insofar as those of us who are not working scientists tend to look toward them as a kind of one-stop problem-solving, question-answering authority. The anonymous 'Scientists have discovered . . .' often provides a sense of reassurance that someone else will figure everything out once and for all. There is no such pretence of anonymous authority in Heidegger's essays: they are very much reflections of *his* thinking, *his* ventures down various paths. Whether or not we care to follow him is ultimately up to us (he certainly does not have an *argument* to the effect that we must care).

Heidegger clearly intends his later writings to cut very much against the grain in terms of how philosophical writing typically looks and what it aspires to achieve. Thus, it is no criticism of his writing to say simply that it 'sounds weird'. Heidegger fully expects that we will be resistant to his writing and to the kind of thinking that writing strives to enact. I would suggest that part of the point of his writing as he does is precisely to make explicit that sense of resistance so that it might be confronted and reflected upon. If we are not simply to rest content with saying that his writing is 'weird', where exactly do the problems lie? If there is something amiss in how he chooses to describe things – simple things like a jug or a bridge,

but also more complex matters like technology and human existence – what is the basis of our criticisms? By what standards are we
measuring the success or failure of his thinking? By leaving this
question unanswered, at least for now, I do not wish to imply that
there are *no* standards for any such measuring, but only that the
question of standards is very much a live one in Heidegger's later philosophy. In particular, he thinks we often go wrong in mixing up our
standards and measures, so that we appeal to science, for example,
as a way of criticizing poetry (a conflation of standards that in some
ways goes all the way back to Plato's *Republic*). So again, just as
Being and Time sought to awaken us to our perplexity, so too do
the later writings seek to foster heightened attention to our own
dispositions and attitudes, our own presuppositions and commitments. The kind of (re)awakening called for in the early philosophy
is very much in demand in the later work as well.

Given the span of Heidegger's later philosophy, there are numerous, diverse pathways to follow him down and it would be folly to
attempt to follow up on all of them in this book. Rather than try to
say a little bit about everything, I want instead to meander down a
small handful of pathways at greater length. I have chosen ones that
I think are central to Heidegger's later philosophy and are also ones
that connect with one another in various ways. Many of these connections are a result of the common origin of several of the writings
we will be examining. Apart from our opening work – 'The Origin
of the Work of Art' – we will be concentrating largely on a cluster
of essays – especially 'The Question Concerning Technology' and
'The Thing' – that began as a series of lectures Heidegger delivered
in Bremen in 1949 in the unlikely venue of a gentlemen's club (owing
to de-Nazification, Heidegger was at the time still barred from
official academic activity; the purpose of these private lectures
was in large part to rehabilitate his standing in German philosophy).
Considering such closely linked writings will facilitate more of a grip
on Heidegger's thinking than trying to follow paths that diverge too
widely. I will thus confess at the outset that there is a great deal of
great import that I am leaving out, such as his four-volume series of
lectures on Nietzsche and his dense and difficult *Beiträge zur
Philosophie* (*Contributions to Philosophy*). My hope, though, is that
by working through what follows, the reader will be well equipped
to follow Heidegger down those paths we have not chosen to take
here.

CHAPTER 9

BEYOND *BEING AND TIME*: 'THE ORIGIN OF THE WORK OF ART'

We can begin working our way into some of the central concepts of Heidegger's later philosophy via a careful examination of Heidegger's lengthy essay from the 1930s, 'The Origin of the Work of Art'. Apart from the intrinsic interest of Heidegger's ideas and insights about art, this essay is especially useful for gauging both the continuities and divergences in Heidegger's thinking as it moves from *Being and Time* into its 'later' period. In terms of points of continuity, the most obvious lies in Heidegger's approach to the question of what art is, which is throughout a question of *what it means to be* a work of art. In this way, Heidegger is again concerned with the question of *being*. Moreover, the specifics of Heidegger's answer to the question of the being of art, of what it means to be a work of art, incorporates continued reflection on many of the concepts and categories that emerged in *Being and Time*, such as *useful things* (equipment), *truth* and *world*. Heidegger's treatment of these now-familiar concepts, however, illustrates the ways in which his thinking is moving beyond *Being and Time*, thereby registering a kind of dissatisfaction with his earlier categories and conclusions. As Heidegger's discussion in this essay makes clear, there is no comfortable location for works of art in the scheme of categories deployed in *Being and Time*, and so that Heidegger is even raising the question of what it means to be a work of art already signals the inadequacy of the ontology of his earlier work. As we will see, however, the inadequacies extend well beyond finding a place for works of art, by means, say, of adding another category while holding the initial ones more or less fixed; on the contrary, *all* of the categories deployed in *Being and Time* will be reconceptualized in the course of this essay, such that no one of them will quite be what it was before. In order to see how Heidegger mounts this rethinking, let us begin where he does, with the rather odd and seemingly narrow question that motivates the entire essay, namely the question of art and its origins.

9A ART AND ORIGINS

One, perhaps rather pedestrian, way to think about the origin of *a* work of art is in more or less causal terms. We might here imagine ourselves at a museum or gallery, standing before a particular painting and asking, 'Where did that come from?' In response, we might then cite various facts about the artist, the time and place of the painting's production, the materials and methods used and so on. In short, we might just read the information on the little cards that accompany paintings and other artworks when they are exhibited. Such information could no doubt be extended in myriad ways, but it would seem that it can serve as at least the beginnings of an answer, with anything else we might add being a matter of detail rather than anything fundamentally different.

As Heidegger makes clear in the very first paragraph of this essay, this causal sense of origins is not the sense that he is asking after in this essay (though it will turn out that there are elements of this sense of 'origins' that provide clues to answering the kind of question he is asking). Heidegger's suggestion is that any such causal account is apt to be incomplete or superficial, since it presupposes that we already have a handle on what in general a work of art *is*. We can see this most easily in the ways in which causal accounts appeal to the activities of an *artist*, which only raises the question of what determines someone as an artist and what makes some activities or processes ones that culminate in works of *art*. Instead, in asking after the origins of the work of art, Heidegger is raising a question of *essence* or *nature*. He is asking what it is about something that, we might say, *makes* it art, and his suggestion is that this kind of question is more basic than, and indeed prior to, any question of origins in the more pedestrian causal sense. In other words, any causal sense of 'origins' takes for granted that we have picked out works of art whose production we might then document. Heidegger's notion of origins concerns what guides us in that initial picking out of something *as* a work of art.

Heidegger's question concerning art's origin, in his specific sense of 'origin', is apt to be met, especially nowadays, with more than a little scepticism. That is, we are likely to see Heidegger's question as somehow invalid or empty, since we tend to think of the question of what art is, like questions of taste more generally, to be more or less a matter of opinion, an ultimately subjective matter not open to critical examination, let alone any kind of definitive answer. Consider on this front the twentieth-century artist Andy Warhol's rather wry, 'Art? That's a man's name', which is an abrupt, albeit witty, dismissal of any question concerning the essence, meaning or definition of art. Attractive (and amusing) as this sceptical response might be, there is something unsatisfying about such a dismissive attitude. After all, we seem to make a distinction between what is and is not art; we use the word 'art' and apply it selectively, and how we apply it would appear to have consequences in terms of how we treat the items to which the word is affixed (or from which it is withheld). Given the nature of our practices, then, we should want to have some clearer understanding of just what is going on in all this distinguishing, labelling and treating. The dismissive response we are now considering would appear to deem all of this distinguishing and labelling to be just that, a kind of affixing of labels where there is nothing more to the notion of a work of art than that it has had the label 'art' affixed to it. To be a work of art is to be labelled a work of art, and how people affix labels will vary in accordance with taste, culture, preference, class and so on. But developing the dismissive response in this way reveals what is most unsatisfying about it, since we are left wondering just what this activity of labelling means or signifies. That is, what are all these people (we) taking something to *be*, when they (we) take it to be *art* (rather than something else)? More succinctly, just what does the label 'art' mean? And when we disagree over when and where to affix this label, what are we disagreeing *about*? If 'art' is to be something more than a mere noise (or simply a man's name), there would appear to be something more to say by way of a definition, so that when we affix the label 'art' we are, rightly or wrongly, saying that what is so labelled belongs to *that* category.

For Heidegger, 'art' is more than an empty label, and he would find any suggestion that it is to be more than disingenuous, as it drastically misrepresents the situation we find ourselves in. That is, we already, all of us, have some sense of art as a distinctive category insofar as we all already distinguish between art and non-art at least to the degree that we can name specific works of art, don't call just any old thing we come across a work of art, value things differently in accordance with whether we consider them works of art or not and so on. By moving in a 'circle' between works of art and the concept of art, Heidegger thinks we can arrive at an answer to the question of origins (again, in his distinctive sense of origins) that is far from empty or dismissive. Here we can see again the role of our 'pre-ontological understanding of being', upon which so much depended in *Being and Time*. That we are already familiar with works of art, can name specific ones when asked, know where to find them if and when we want: all of this shows already that there is more to be said than the sceptical, dismissive response would allow. Indeed, that we all know at least some *things* that are works of art provides a promising clue, according to Heidegger: all works of art have, he says, a 'thingly' character. If we can get clear about things, then we might be able to figure out what it is about some things that makes them works of art.

9B THINGS, EQUIPMENT AND WORKS

That Heidegger proposes approaching the question of what works of art are via first reflecting more generally on the notion of a *thing* is apt to strike the careful reader of *Being and Time* as a rather surprising strategy. After all, in that earlier work, Heidegger had invoked the notion of a thing (or 'mere things') at the outset of his phenomenology of everydayness, but only as an ill-conceived response to the question of what Da-sein encounters in its day-to-day activity. The notion of a thing in *Being and Time* had thus played the role of foil for the ultimately more enlightened description of what we encounter as an array of handy useful things, an inter-related constellation of equipment pervaded and sustained by myriad referential relations. Now, however, the 'mere thing' is no longer a notion to be spurned as the kind of initially empty category that gets filled in by more materialistically minded philosophers; on the contrary, Heidegger's treatment of the notion of a thing in 'The Origin of the Work of Art' marks the beginning of a decades-long exploration that serves as a centrepiece for his later philosophy as a whole. (Here is one place where 'The Origin of the Work of Art' serves as a kind of 'gateway' onto the later Heidegger: at several places, themes and ideas are announced that will be developed in considerably more detail in subsequent decades.)

Even leaving aside the negative role the notion of a thing was cast in previously in Heidegger's philosophy, the notion hardly seems promising as a way of getting clearer about something as specific as works of art. As Heidegger himself acknowledges, the notion of a thing is incredibly general, so much so that one might wonder whether it constitutes any kind of category at all. We use the notion of a thing to talk about individual items, as when we say, 'Hand me that *thing* over there, will you?' and 'There's the *thing* I was talking about yesterday', but there are also uses where 'thing' does not pick out a discrete entity, certainly not one that is readily demarcated in spatial terms. Love, after all, is a many-splendoured *thing*, or we say, 'The *thing* is, I don't really like slasher movies', while the eschatalogically minded among us may find themselves worried about 'last *things*'. *Thing* thus seems to be more or less a placeholder, to be used to designate pretty much anything (there it is again) that can be talked about, pointed to, mentioned, argued over, worried about and so on. That there is any kind of unity to this notion thus seems questionable, to say the least. How, then, is the appeal to the notion of a thing (where a coffee cup, passing thought, matter of concern or even a notion itself can be a thing) likely to get us anywhere in thinking about what works of art are?

Heidegger argues that we can cut through this haze of generality by concentrating on the sense of 'thing' at work in the phrase, 'mere thing', where the general connotation *is* one of designating an individual entity. This narrower sense of 'thing' brings us into the neighbourhood of the seemingly synonymous notion of an *object*. Though this latter notion likewise suffers from some of the same hazy generality (witness 'the *object* of my affections'), the central use would appear to be more well defined. (Appearances may be misleading, however, since the notion of an object may be harder to pin down than it might initially seem and, moreover, we may go wrong in hastily assimilating the notion of a thing to that of an object. The latter point is one that Heidegger himself makes on many occasions.)

Heidegger explores three traditional conceptions of 'mere things', none of which he finds to be satisfactory or satisfying in capturing what is 'thingly' about things. The first and second conceptions all but obliterate the thingly character of things; the third conception, however, at least points us in the right direction. The three conceptions are:

1. The thing is to be understood as a bearer of properties. On this conception, the thing serves as a kind of logical unity or unifier, the X to which various properties are ascribed or in which various properties inhere. My coffee cup is a thing, which is to say that it is something, some thing, that supports or bears the properties of being white, being ceramic, holding hot liquids and so on.

Heidegger's complaint about this conception is that it holds the thing at a distance, since we never apprehend the bearer, the core, but only the properties. (Take away all the qualities of my coffee cup, and what is there any longer to apprehend?)

2. The thing is to be understood as the unity of a sensible manifold. This second conception might be understood as a response to the 'disappearance' of the thing that occurs in thinking through the first conception. That is, since we never come across or apprehend the X underlying all of these properties, but only the properties or qualities themselves, then the thing is really nothing more than this collection of properties. Such a conception banishes any mysterious appeal to an underlying I-know-not-what that somehow holds together or 'supports' the perceived qualities of the thing; rather, the thing just is those perceived qualities, taken collectively.

Heidegger again finds this conception wanting, and in more than one way. One complaint he raises is phenomenological in nature (indeed, he repeats a point he had stressed earlier, in *Being and Time* – see BT, p. 153/163–4), since this conception seems to be inaccurate to our experience. That is, our perceptual experience is not by and large, and certainly not primarily, directed toward perceptible qualities (we do not, Heidegger says, first perceive a 'throng of sensations'). Rather, our perceptions are from the start more thingly in nature: we hear the *truck* going past, not a noise that we then interpret as the noise of a truck by, say, binding it to other qualities we apprehend.

Heidegger's second complaint parallels the kind of complaint he raised against the first conception: whereas the first conception ultimately leads to a disappearance of the thing by making the thing too remote (the X that properties inhere in, but is only apprehended via an apprehension of those properties and never directly), this second conception marks the thing's disappearance by bringing it too close. The thing is *nothing more* than the perceptions we have of it, but this fails to do justice to the sense of 'self-containment' we accord to the thing, as something 'out there' to be perceived, perhaps, but not just our perceptions.

3. The thing is to be understood as formed matter (matter and form). By appealing explicitly to the notion of materiality, this third conception would appear to avoid the problems Heidegger detects in the first two conceptions. As material in nature, the thing is thereby accorded a kind of bodily density and separateness that the first two conceptions threatened to efface. Moreover, the appeal to *form* accords with the idea that a thing is an individual, set apart from its surroundings, capable of being named and numbered as a particular, discrete entity.

This third conception seems especially promising for thinking about works of art, since the work of the artist would appear to be one of forming, or imposing a form onto, matter. This is especially evident in sculpture, where the sculptor fashions the raw material so that it takes on a specific shape.

Heidegger notes that the notion of form is complicated, as it involves at least two different ideas. Consider, for example, a rock found lying on the ground out in the woods or by a river. Such a rock is an ideal candidate for being a mere thing: it is an individual, material entity, naturally occurring without any preordained use, purpose or significance. It is, we might say, just a rock and nothing more (this is not to say that it cannot be put to some use, as when I use it to scare off a lurking bear, open some nuts I brought on my hike for a snack, take it home to use as a paperweight and so on, but all of these uses are secondary to the nature and existence of the rock itself, which was after all lying there, and would have remained lying there, had I not come along and put it to use). As just a rock, and as a mere thing, its *form* would appear to be nothing more than its more or less accidental shape; the form, in other words, signifies little more than the distribution of the matter making up the rock. But this minimal notion of form is certainly not what is in play in thinking about other kinds of things, in particular items of equipment and works of art. In the latter categories, the notion of form is far from accidental. The form of the hammer is not just the way the matter happens to be distributed, likewise for the statue or painting; the form here is not so much the distribution of matter as what determines the distribution of matter. In this way, form is *prior* to matter, since the matter would not be distributed in this manner were it not for the form.

This richer, more determinative conception of form raises a further problem, however. If we try to elaborate upon or explicate this idea of determination, then, in the case of useful things or equipment at least, we have a fairly clear idea of how to proceed: the determinative character of the form is bound up with the equipment's use, with what the equipment is *for*. For example, the coffee cup is shaped in the way that it is so as to hold liquids in a manner that is effective for carrying and drinking; the hammer has the form it has to be of use for hammering in (and often pulling out) nails. This appeal to use, function and purpose, while applying quite comfortably to the category of equipment, applies much more awkwardly, if at all, to works of art. If we ask the question of what works of art are *for*, what purpose they serve or use they have, nothing springs readily to mind, as there does not appear to be any obvious task or job that a work of art is made to fulfil. (One might say that works of art do the job of providing aesthetic pleasure, but that strikes me as a rather forced, artificial kind of use.) There seems to be something self-sufficient or self-contained about the work of art, in that it does not have any obvious use or purpose beyond itself (it does not appear to be caught up in the 'referential totality' the way equipment is). At the same time, the work of art is also something formed in the more determinative sense, and so would appear to be something intermediate between mere things and items of equipment (things of use).

These ruminations thus far do not seem to get us very far in getting clear about the notion of a thing, let alone the work of art. Indeed, Heidegger thinks that all three conceptions of what a thing is, even the most promising one of formed matter, are all ultimately 'assaults' on the thing. All three conceptions turn out to be procrustean, in the sense that one has to force things into their categories, by pushing the thing away (i), falsifying our experience of the thing (ii) or assimilating things, equipment and works (iii). Rather than categorize or conceptualize in this manner, the important thing is to let things be, to let them be the things that they are. This may sound easy, but Heidegger thinks that talking about things in a way that respects and preserves their thingly character is actually extremely difficult.

Despite the largely negative conclusions reached thus far, Heidegger thinks that with proper sifting and sorting, clues for a more positive line of thought can be found. In particular, many of the considerations raised in relation to the notion of a thing as formed matter appear to be particularly promising. The danger there was one of assimilating artworks with equipment, which is hampered by the lack of any obvious use or purpose on the part of works of art. In spite of this danger, Heidegger thinks that it may nonetheless be worthwhile to reflect further on the thingly character of equipment, since it is after all something familiar and readily accessible (especially in light of the work done by *Being and Time*) and such further reflections may prove illuminating for the thingly character of the work of art, if only by contrast or counterpoint.

Equipment is always to be understood as something for something. As being for something, items of equipment thus serve some purpose within the context of ongoing activity, and so have a place within that activity. (Again, these points are familiar from Heidegger's explication of useful things in *Being and Time*: the same German word, *Zeug*, which Stambaugh translates as 'useful things' and Macquarrie and Robinson translate as 'equipment', is used in this essay.) Every useful thing, as embedded in the referential totality constitutive of worldliness, 'refers', as Heidegger puts it, to that world, though not in any explicit sense. A hammer does not refer to nails, lumber and so on in the sense of saying or announcing anything explicitly about those things. Indeed, quite the opposite: another important aspect of Heidegger's account of equipment in *Being and Time* is its tendency, when used, to 'withdraw'. A principal virtue of equipment is that it *not* be noticed or attended to when it is most properly working as the equipment that it is (usually, Heidegger thinks, we only notice equipment when something has gone wrong, when the item of equipment we need is broken or missing, when an unneeded item of equipment is in the way or when we have stopped our work and devote ourselves to idle looking about).

This tendency toward transparency and withdrawal means that items of equipment are not particularly useful for revealing themselves, i.e. for revealing the kinds of things they are. Heidegger's carefully chosen example is a peasant's shoes, which play a very specific and important role in the life of the peasant. The shoes protect the peasant's feet, allowing her to carry on in her toil; they may have a look or style that marks them out as belonging to this particular region and time; the shoes bear the traces of the peasant's labours, wearing down in ways that reflect her gait and tread, soiled with the earth upon which the peasant walks, ageing with the passing seasons that mark the cycle of her work and rest. While the shoes are constituted by their role in the life of the peasant and at the same time reflect or bear the traces of that life, the actual shoes do not call attention to that role, nor to the life in which they have that role. As equipment, they are simply used, worn, cared for and eventually replaced in the ongoing life of the peasant. While the shoes might be 'read' so as to explicate the life and world of the peasant, any such reading is not part and parcel of the ongoing use of the shoes.

Now consider one of van Gogh's paintings of peasant shoes. Unlike actual shoes, which withdraw insofar as they are put to use, the shoes in the painting are there precisely to be noticed, to be gazed at, indeed to be read. Recall Heidegger's remark in *Being and Time* regarding hammers, namely that 'the less we just stare at the thing called hammer, the more actively we use it, the more original our relation to it becomes and the more undisguisedly it is encountered as what it is, as a useful thing [as equipment]' (BT, p. 65/69). Such a remark could easily be applied to the peasant's shoes: the less they are stared at and the more they are instead worn, the more primordial is the peasant's relation to them. But now consider the shoes in the painting: there is here no possibility of taking hold of them, of putting them to use in the manner that real shoes are; moreover, the whole point of the shoes in the painting is to be *looked at* (staring may not be quite right, as that term arouses connotations of blankness), to be taken in visually and so do anything but withdraw (a painting whose goal is to be unnoticed is a very odd sort of painting). By holding forth the shoes, so that they do not withdraw but are instead explicitly noticed, the painting announces something about the shoes, so that we notice the shoes and their place in the life of those who wear them. The painting, Heidegger says, lets 'us know what the shoes, in truth, are' (OBT, p. 15). All of those aspects of the life of the shoes, and so the life of those who wear them, which the real shoes bore without making manifest, are made manifest in the painting. Heidegger quickly concludes from this that 'the essential nature of art would then be this: the setting-itself-to-work of the truth of beings' (OBT, p. 16).

9C ART AND WORLD

Heidegger's contention that the nature of art is 'the setting-itself-to-work of the truth of beings' allows for a wide range of possibilities in terms of the scope of 'the truth of beings', as well as the way that truth 'sets itself to work'. In what I regard as Heidegger's preliminary examples – the van Gogh painting of the shoes, Meyer's poem, 'Roman Fountain' – what is brought to a stand, i.e. allowed to shine forth, is the truth of a particular (kind of) entity. The van Gogh painting shows us 'what shoes, in truth, are', which means that the painting makes the being of the shoes manifest to and for those of us who view the painting. (That those of us viewing the painting are by and large outsiders to the life and world of the peasant is the principal reason why this example is a preliminary one; I will return to this point shortly.) Heidegger's subsequent discussion expands considerably the scope of 'the truth of beings', so that what a work of art makes manifest is not the being of this or that entity, but precisely the truth of *beings*, what there is as a whole. This is not at all to say that a work of art depicts, or attempts to depict, everything there is in the way that van Gogh's painting depicts a pair of shoes. Indeed, Heidegger warns us against fixating on the notion of depiction or representing as indicative of the essential nature of art (what Heidegger regards as among the greatest works of art turn out not to be pictorial or representational at all). So what then might it mean to say that a work of art is the truth of beings *as a whole* setting itself to work? If we reach way back to the opening pages of *Being and Time*, we can there find a clue to what Heidegger has in mind. Recall Heidegger's preliminary formulation of the meaning of being: 'What is *asked about* in the question to be elaborated is being, that which determines beings as beings, that in terms of which beings have always been understood no matter how they are discussed' (BT, pp. 4–5/6). As before in *Being and Time*, both of these aspects – determination and understanding – are involved in what Heidegger here discusses primarily under the rubric of 'the truth of beings'. We can discern the connection when Heidegger says that when 'the truth of the being has set itself to work' in the work of art, 'the being of the being comes into the constancy of its shining' (OBT, p. 16).

To speak of the being of beings involves how entities are understood and how they are determined as beings. If a work of art is 'the setting-itself-to-work of the truth of beings', that means that a work of art sets up or installs an understanding of being, and so in some way allows to 'shine forth' how entities are determined as entities. This is no doubt still pretty obscure, so it might be best to work toward these ideas via Heidegger's central example: the Greek temple. Notice first that Heidegger says that the Greek temple 'portrays nothing', which marks a difference from the van Gogh example. Thus, however it is that the temple sets truth to work, it is not by means of representing or picturing anything (this in turn indicates that the truth of beings set forth in a work of art is not to be understood in terms of how entities look). The second thing to note is what might be called the site-specificity of the temple: 'Standing there, the building rests on the rocky ground' (OBT, p. 21). As resting on the ground, the temple thus belongs to a particular region. The notion of belonging signifies more than just where the temple happens to be: it is *of* the region where it is, by being 'installed' there (and only there), and it is of the region in the further sense of being crafted out of the material found there.

The site-specificity of the temple pertains not just to the way the temple is located in a particular region, but to its being located with respect to a particular *people*, a culture for whom the temple holds significance. But these ways of putting things, that the temple belongs to a people and to a region, are for Heidegger more or less backwards: 'But men and animals, plants and things, are never present and familiar as unalterable things fortuitously constituting a suitable environment for the temple that, one day, is added to what is already present' (OBT, p. 21). Heidegger thus wants to claim that the temple, as a work of art, is what first allows there to be a region and a people. To begin with the latter, let us consider the following dense passage:

> The temple and its precinct do not, however, float off into the indefinite. It is the temple work that first structures and simultaneously gathers around itself the unity of those paths and relations in which birth and death, disaster and blessing, victory and disgrace, endurance and decline acquire for the human being the shape of destiny. (OBT, pp. 20–1)

Heidegger's talk here of 'fitting together' and 'gathering' is crucial for understanding his conception of the 'work' done by a work of art. The suggestion here is that it is only by means of the temple that the 'paths and relations' of a people become a unity, so that it makes sense to speak of *a* people, culture or nation at all. 'Standing there, the temple first gives to things their look, and to men their outlook on themselves' (OBT, p. 21). We can hear in this claim an echo of the twofold explication of the notion of being that Heidegger offers in *Being and Time*: to say that the temple 'gives to things their look' means that the temple sets up a way for entities to be ('determines entities as entities'), but at the same time, by giving human beings an 'outlook on themselves', the temple establishes an understanding, both a kind of self-understanding and an understanding of things (in terms of the 'look' given them by the temple). The work of art provides a 'measure', which again has a twofold significance, in the sense of both the activity of measuring (getting the measure of something, and so in that way understanding it) and things measured (the thing is determined as something in virtue of its being so measured).

The temple 'fits together' and 'gathers around itself' the 'paths and relations' of a group of people so that they might be more than just a mere group and so that the events in their lives may be more than just a series of things that befall them. Heidegger's examples of birth and death, disaster and blessing and so on suggest that the temple gathers together and so sets up meaningful differences in terms of which things matter (and matter in particular ways) to a people. The temple, as giving things their 'look', opens up a 'view' that 'remains open as long as the work is a work, as long as the god has not fled from it' (OBT, p. 21). Heidegger refers to this 'open view', this 'opening' afforded by the work, as the establishment of a *world*: 'As a work, the work holds open the open of a world' (OBT, p. 23). Without the work done by the work of art, in this case the Greek temple, there would not be such a world, such a way in which people understand themselves and what surrounds them. We need to keep in mind here that by 'world' Heidegger intends something along the lines of the sense he developed in *Being and Time* in his account of Da-sein as being-in-the-world:

World is not a mere collection of the things – countable and uncountable, known and unknown – that are present at hand.

116

Neither is world a merely imaginary framework added by our representation to the sum of things that are present. *World worlds*, and is more fully in being than all those tangible and perceptible things in the midst of which we take ourselves to be at home. (OBT, p. 23)

To say that 'world worlds' does not mean that a collection of objects continues to exist through time, but that there is a way in which what exists is *understood*, that there are people who stay 'in the openness of beings' (OBT, p. 23). We can thus think of world here as something like a space of intelligibility (Heidegger often refers to such a space as an 'open' or 'clearing'), wherein things are manifest or show up, and do so in particular, distinctive ways.

To say that the work of art sets truth to work means that the work opens up and sustains such a world. By 'fitting together' and 'gathering', the work organizes and unifies what would otherwise be a disparate, haphazard collection of activities and practices, again just a bunch of stuff people (and other animals) do. The 'truth of beings' thus refers to the entire 'look' given to entities by means of the work of art. Heidegger's talk of fitting and gathering can be understood as operating at several levels, from the quite concrete or literal to something more diffuse and abstract. Concretely, the temple gathers people by being a site around which their activities are organized. The temple might serve as the place where births and deaths are acknowledged by means of ceremonies that give those events their particular 'look', prayers may be offered at the temple for victory in battle, apologies and offerings made in light of defeat and so on. The temple thus gathers people together quite literally, brings their activities into alignment with one another, so that they make up a people. In doing so, the temple thereby gathers together their understanding of things, imposing a unity of meaning or significance on the events making up their lives – the birth of a child has *this* significance; victory in battle *this* meaning; the coming of Spring *this* relevance; and so on – so that they are delineated or determined as those discrete events.

Heidegger's equating of the truth of beings with the setting or opening up of a world suggests that the truth of beings is something that has a *history*, something that changes over time (this is perhaps the most significant departure from the outlook and aspirations of *Being and Time* and its ideal of 'fundamental ontology').

Heidegger's juxtaposition of the Greek temple, an ancient work of art, with his example of the Medieval cathedral helps to bring out this idea. Each of these sets up or installs very different ways of understanding what there is; each of these sets up a different world, but this should not be understood as 'a merely imaginary framework added by our representation to the sum of things that are present' (OBT, p. 23). What things there are – how entities are determined as entities – is itself something that changes. Consider the kind of meaningful differences that might be gathered and articulated by the cathedral: saint and sinner, damnation and salvation, Heaven and Hell, eternal and worldly and so on. Many of these will find no real counterpart in the world of the ancient Greeks, and even those that do will take on a very different look. For an example where no real counterpart is available, in what sense could someone in the world of the Greek temple *be* a sinner (or saint)? In what sense can someone living in the world opened up by the cathedral *be* a hero? Nothing – no one – shows up as a sinner in the Greek world, and what might have looked heroic or exalted in the Greek world looks proud and sinful in the world of the cathedral. Again, this should not be understood as the imposing of an 'imagined framework' onto what are otherwise the same events. A hero and a sinner are not the same people differently understood, as though it were a matter of sticking a different tag or label on, but entirely different ways to be. And even where there appear to be counterparts or overlap among the meaningful differences articulated and sustained by the two different works of art, there are serious limitations on the degree of overlap: what look like more or less the same events may have wildly different meanings or significance. Compare the significance of birth and death for those whose lives are gathered and unified by the temple and those who live in the world of the cathedral: could an ancient Greek baby be born with original sin? While that question might make sense for those living in the world opened by the cathedral, it is not a question that could have meaningfully arisen (let alone have had an answer) in the world of the Greeks.

The work of art 'opens up a *world* and keeps it abidingly in force' (OBT, p. 22), which means that a work of art establishes and sustains a way in which things make sense, an opening or clearing. Heidegger's provocative claim is that there could not be such openings or clearings without works of art, without something that serves to gather together and unify, and so in that sense focus, the 'paths and relations' of people so as to amount to an understanding of being: 'The openness of this open, i.e., truth, can only be what it is, namely, *this* open, when and as long as it establishes itself in its open. In this open, therefore, there must be a being in which the openness takes its stand and achieves constancy' (OBT, p. 36). At this point, it should be relatively clear why I claimed that the van Gogh example must only be a preliminary one (though Heidegger never explicitly labels it as one). While the painting may show to us what 'shoes are in truth', and even in that way afford some insight into the world in which those shoes have their place (their particular use and significance), the painting plays no role *in* that world, i.e. it does not establish or hold open that world for those whose world it is. Thus, while we can appreciate Heidegger's point that the life of the ancient Greeks would not be *that* life without the temple, one would be hard-pressed to make a similar claim concerning the life of the peasant and van Gogh's painting. The painting does not first give 'to things their look and to men their outlook on themselves', certainly not if the 'men' we are considering are those whose world is made manifest by means of the painting (it could be that the distinctive style of van Gogh and other kindred painters fits together and so gathers the 'paths and relations' of those for whom the paintings are produced, but Heidegger does not pursue this idea). While the painting may gather things together for *us*, those of us who view the painting and take the time to 'read' it in the right way, it does nothing to gather the 'paths and relations' of the peasants whose lives are brought into view by the painting.

9D WORLD AND EARTH

Given the conception of the work of art Heidegger develops, especially via the example of the Greek temple, his opening gambit of reviewing and criticizing various philosophical conceptions of the notion of a *thing* may now appear to be more or less irrelevant, a kind of opening exercise that led to nothing but a dead end. Such an appearance is misleading, however, as there are still clues lurking in those conceptions of a thing, despite their ultimately problematic, even 'violent', character. In particular, the third conception, that of the thing as 'formed matter', is worth reconsidering in light of the idea that the work of art is 'the truth of beings setting itself to work'. If we consider Heidegger's claim that the work of art opens up and sustains a world, that it 'gathers' the 'paths and relations' of human beings and thereby gives 'to things their look and to men their outlook on themselves', all of this serves to specify a kind of function, purpose or role for works of art. That there is something works of art *do* gives us a richer conception of *form* than mere distribution of matter, but without assimilating works of art to the category of equipment (where a functional notion of form quite readily applies). Works of art do not 'work' the way equipment does, i.e. they do not 'withdraw' or become transparent in their functioning; that they do not withdraw indicates that their role is, we might say, *ontological* in the sense that the work done by works of art pertains to the opening of a *world*, rather than accomplishing this or that task within some already-formed world of activity (hammers and nails belong to a world, but they do not open up and sustain one).

While we can understand how the notion of form foreshadows Heidegger's conception of art, what is missing from the account thus far developed is the fate of the notion of *matter*. What is missing, in other words, is attention to the materiality, and so the full thingliness, of the work of art. The materiality of works of art is by no means an accidental feature of them, according to Heidegger, but essential to how works of art work and what they reveal or make manifest. That is, the materiality of works of art reveals something about the very idea of a world, of what it means for one to be 'opened' and 'sustained', as well as the limits to those notions. The materiality of works of art signals the interplay between world and what Heidegger here calls *earth*. The appearance of earth as a kind of counterpart and constraint on the notion of world marks another important reconception of the categories of *Being and Time*. In that early work, there is, to be sure, something outside of or beyond Dasein's world, but it is only 'de-worlded' stuff, the objectively present, which is first revealed in moments of breakdown and episodes of idle staring and which can be reconceived by means of the theoretical models of the natural sciences; there is, however, none of the interplay between Da-sein's world(s) and the objectively present that Heidegger here ascribes to world and earth. Moreover, earth, as Heidegger develops it here, is not what the natural sciences study and theorize about, but instead something more like what *resists* any attempt at theorizing. These points will emerge more clearly as we proceed.

Earth and world make their first appearance as paired concepts in the following passage, where Heidegger is still considering the category of equipment: 'This equipment belongs *to the earth* and finds protection in the *world* of the peasant woman. From out of this protected belonging the equipment itself rises to its resting-within-itself' (OBT, p. 14). Even in equipment there is something 'earthy' as well as 'worldly'. Equipment is worldly insofar as its functionality is a matter of its being integrated into some human way of life, the various practices for putting it to various, and variously proper, uses. But equipment is also materially real, made of various materials and liable to natural events and processes. Equipment wears out over time, breaks and decays, and in so doing has a way of 'receding' back into the earth. (At least equipment used to do this, before the advent of such a bewildering array of 'synthetic' materials. Even these have at least some 'earthy' character, but their appearance may signal a kind of loss of what Heidegger refers to here as 'belonging', a danger he associates with the rise of our current scientific-technological understanding of being. More on this shortly.)

Heidegger continues the passage just cited concerning earth and world with the observation that 'perhaps it is only in the picture that we notice all this about the shoes' (OBT, p. 14). Again, the suggestion is that the work of art makes something manifest that would otherwise pass unnoticed. In this instance, what is noticed is not just the life of the shoes, the life in which the shoes have their life, but the way the shoes, and the entire life to which they belong, are *grounded*, both literally and figuratively, in a materially real setting. This idea of grounding is further exemplified in the example of the Greek temple, whose 'site-specificity' underscores the way in which the temple, in opening up a particular human world, is based in a particular natural-material setting that is the basis too of the world sustained by the temple. Indeed, Heidegger claims that it is the presence of the temple that first delineates and articulates this earthy surrounding. The temple 'makes visible' its natural and material setting; it 'lights up that on which and in which man bases his dwelling' (OBT, p. 21). The work of art 'sets up a world'. In doing so, it also 'sets forth the earth'. Heidegger refers to these as the 'two essential traits' of a work of art:

> The setting up of a world and the setting forth of earth are two
> essential traits belonging to the work-being of the work. Within

the unity of that work-being, however, they belong together. This unity is what we we seek when we reflect on the self-sufficiency of the work and try to express in words the closed, unitary repose of this resting-in-itself. (OBT, p. 26)

Heidegger's insistence on the 'unity' of the 'work-being' is meant to emphasize that these two 'essential features' should not be thought of as separate tasks accomplished by the work of art. They are instead far more intertwined and interconnected: 'In setting up a world, the work sets forth the earth' (OBT, p. 24). By doing one, the work of art thereby does the other as well.

But what it is about a work of art that 'sets forth the earth'? Indeed, what does Heidegger really have in mind in this appeal to earth at all? To begin with the second question, we have already seen that Heidegger intends the notion of earth to name the idea that any human world, any space of intelligibility, is situated in a materially real and materially specific setting. This is indicated in the first part of the following: 'World is grounded on earth, and earth rises up through world' (OBT, p. 26). The idea of grounding is literal, in the sense that different spaces of intelligibility, i.e. different epochs in the understanding of being, emerged in, and so incorporated, many features of a particular earthy environment. But there is a deeper sense that Heidegger intends here as well. Every space of intelligibility, every world, as an understanding of what there is as a whole, provides a kind of opening on everything there is. Whatever there is shows up or is manifest in accordance with the shape of that particular understanding of being. (Again, compare the way human actions are manifest in an ancient Greek understanding of being versus how they show up in a Medieval Christian understanding.) There is always, however, something ultimately procrustean about any such understanding: beings as a whole are revealed, but only in accordance with a particular way of understanding. In being revealed in some respects, beings are at the same time concealed in others. Earth, for Heidegger, names this way in which what there is escapes or even resists the various attempts at human understanding:

The earth is openly illuminated as itself only where it is apprehended and preserved as the essentially undisclosable, as that which withdraws from every disclosure, in other words, keeps itself constantly closed up. (OBT, p. 25)

The earth is 'undisclosable' in that it forms a kind of basis or back-drop for making sense (a world just is a unified way of making sense of things), but as a basis or backdrop, it eludes the sense-making activities it grounds. Such elusiveness further speaks to the *vulner-ability* of any historical understanding of being. Earth 'rises up through world' in the sense that every space of intelligibility is inher-ently finite, indeed mortal, an opening onto things that will someday close. (Here again we see Heidegger's existential conception of death at work: much of what he says about Da-sein and death in *Being and Time* can be transposed to this more cultural-historical level. Cultures, and not just individuals, are pervaded by an indelible finitude, though cultures, like individuals, may not readily face up to this.) World and earth are thus in opposition to one another: every world, as a clearing, clears away some part of the earth. Any such clearing requires effort and exertion – ground must be cleared, raw materials variously mined, felled, smelted, moulded, fired, hewn and harvested – and whatever clearing has been done remains vulner-able to its environment (iron is vulnerable to rust, wood to rot and ter-mites, and so on). A world imposes itself on the earth, and while the earth accommodates this imposition, it resists it as well. In talking of an opposition between world and earth, however, Heidegger does not wish to depict their relation in entirely dark or negative terms:

> The opposition of world and earth is strife. We would, to be sure, all too easily falsify the essence of the strife were we to conflate that essence with discord and dispute, and to know it, therefore, only as disruption and destruction. In essential strife, however, the opponents raise each other into the self-assertion of their essences. (OBT, p. 26)

Though it is tempting to read Heidegger's contrast between earth and world as his way of articulating a rather standard opposition between *nature* and *culture*, his characterization of that contrast as involving 'striving' suggests that we should not give in to that temp-tation too easily. The interplay between earth and world is, for Heidegger, far more complicated than the standard opposition would allow. According to the standard model, nature simply is what it is, regardless of whether there is any (human) culture at all; this in turn suggests that culture is always ultimately a kind of imposition upon nature. The intimacy of the relation between world and earth, such that the earth 'shelters' the world while at the same resisting the world's attempt to render everything intelligible in its terms, is much more subtle and nuanced than simple opposition. Any world is always 'earthy', as something built upon and resisted by the earth, but Heidegger also suggests that the earth is also always worldly, insofar as the earth can only be manifest as earth in its particular striving with a particular world.

To return now to the first question – what is it about a work of art that 'sets forth the earth'? – a work of art plays a distinctive role in this interplay between earth and world: 'The work moves the earth into the open of a world and holds it there. *The work lets the earth be an earth*' (OBT, p. 24). We have already developed this notion via the example of the Greek temple, whose emergence first delineates the surrounding environment precisely *as* that environment. But this delineation and articulation is not just a matter of what surrounds the work, but is something inherent in the work itself. Again, a work of art is something materially real, matter that has been worked over, and so formed. A work of art, like items of equipment, uses raw materials. However, there is once again a useful contrast to be drawn between equipment and works of art. In the case of equipment, the raw materials are used in such a way as to disappear: 'In the manufacture of equipment – for example, an ax – the stone is used and used up. It disappears into usefulness' (OBT, p. 24). Equipment thus does not 'let the earth be an earth' in any meaningful sense, because nothing conspicuously earthy remains in the finished item of equipment.

Heidegger's account of the materiality of equipment here in 'The Origin of the Work of Art' is importantly different from the lengthy account in *Being and Time* in the following respect. In *Being and Time*, there was no place in the phenomenology of everydayness for anything categorically distinct from useful things, save for Da-sein itself. Prior to any kind of breakdown situation, wherein the unhandy and the objectively present are encountered, Heidegger claims that *everything* shows up in terms of usefulness. The strained character of this claim is evident in the following passage, where he asserts that even the raw materials used to produce equipment are to be understood in terms of usefulness:

A reference to 'materials' is contained in the work at the same time. The work is dependent upon leather, thread, nails, and similar things. Leather in its turn is produced from hides. These hides are taken from animals which were bred and raised by others. We also find animals in the world which were not bred and raised and even when they have been raised these beings produce themselves in a certain sense. Thus beings are accessible in the surrounding world which in themselves do not need to be produced and are always already at hand. Hammer, tongs, nails in themselves refer to – they consist of – steel, iron, metal, stone, wood. 'Nature' is also discovered in the use of useful things, 'nature' in the light of products of nature. (BT, p. 66/70)

Heidegger continues by noting that 'nature must not be understood here as what is merely objectively present, nor as the *power of nature*. The forest is a forest of timber, the mountain a quarry of rock, the river is water power, the wind is wind "in the sails" ' (BT, p. 66/70). The equipmental character of everyday experience is pervasive and without exception. There is nothing in everyday experience that in any way exceeds or resists being viewed as useful or handy (ready-to-hand), even what belongs to 'Nature'. Note the difference in Heidegger's characterization of equipment in 'The Origin of the Work of Art', when he says that the peasant's shoes, for example, belong 'to the *earth*'. There is no such belonging in *Being and Time*, since anything 'earthy' about equipment in his earlier account remains within the referential totality, the system of references or assignments that constitute the category of useful things. Hence, the materiality of equipment in *Being and Time* involves nothing 'self-secluding', let alone 'undisclosable'. The introduction of the notion of earth as a counterpart to world marks an important and far-reaching change in Heidegger's philosophy: the idea of something that grounds, and yet resists, the understanding of being plays an important role in his worries concerning our current technological understanding of being. (Again, more on this below.)

In contrast to equipment, the work of art uses raw materials but, in keeping with its essentially conspicuous character, it uses them without using them up. The materiality of the raw materials used in the work is itself made manifest: 'On the other hand, the temple work, in setting up a world, does not let the material disappear; rather, it allows it to come forth for the very first time, to come forth, that is, into the open of the world of the work' (OBT, p. 24). The work of art displays, rather than hides, the materiality of what composes it: the colours and textures of the painted canvas; the mass and density of the carved rock; the sonority of the musical notes; the rhythm and tone of the poem's words. Notice in particular how Heidegger characterizes the 'coming forth' of the earth in the work of art, namely, that it comes 'into the open of the world of the work'. This way of putting it is in keeping with his more general insistence that the two 'essential features' of a work of art constitute a unity. The coming forth of the earth is not a separate moment of the working of a work of art, but part and parcel of the work's 'setting up a world'. This unity is especially evident in the *interplay* of earth and world in the work of art. The already noted oppositional character of earth and world is not just depicted or made manifest in the work of art, but, in keeping with the founding role of the work of art in 'setting up a world', the work *instigates* the opposition between world and earth. In a work of art, form and matter are intimately and intricately related. The matter is worked (clay is moulded, rock is carved, paints are brushed, smeared and daubed, sounds are arranged, combined and controlled), but not in such a way that the materiality of the work is hidden or effaced. The matter of the work 'rises through' the work, thereby exemplifying and instigating the earth's jutting through the particular world set up by the work. As requiring work, the form is indeed imposed on the matter, but in a way that allows the matter to remain manifest both *as* matter and *as* resisting the imposition of form.

The 'strife' Heidegger speaks of is this back and forth of imposition and resistance. This strife, moreover, has to be understood not as a kind of general condition, but something that a founding work of art such as the temple or the cathedral instigates in a very particular way. That is, the strife instigated by a work of art is particular to the world set up by the work. This is to be expected, as every world embodies a particular understanding of being, a particular 'truth of beings', and so both the way the earth is set forth and the way the earth resists that way of understanding pertain uniquely to that world. The strife between the temple and its environs is different from that between the cathedral and its ground: each uses matter differently, and so each makes manifest a different opposition between world and earth. For example, what resists the world of the temple may be the inarticulate surge of *phusis*, which is exemplified in the temple's relation to the surrounding sea: 'The steadfastness of the work stands out against the surge of the tide, and, in its own repose, brings out the raging of the surf' (OBT, p. 21). In the case of the cathedral, by contrast, the vaults and archways that gather together the understanding of things heavenly and divine are resisted by the ground's earthly pull, which is emphasized all the more by the loftiness of the structure.

9E CREATORS AND PRESERVERS

The particularity of the opposition between world and earth instigated by a work of art is also evident in the way that opposition may by and large *cease*. A work of art may go dead, not in the sense that it ceases to exist or even that it no longer has such admirable qualities as beauty, elegance or intricate design, but rather in the sense that it no longer stands in the middle of a world founded by it. Insofar as a work of art creates and sustains an 'opening' onto beings, any such opening may at the same time close over once again: the ancient Greek understanding of being is no longer available, in that it is no longer inhabitable by anyone (it can, to be sure, remain an object of study, but only from the outside). Similarly for the Medieval cathedral: even though the practice of Christianity persists, life is no longer gathered together in the all-encompassing way it was for Medieval Christians. The world opened up by our current understanding of being is no longer (only) a testimony to God's glory, where every element speaks to the order and significance of the Creation. Our world is one now articulated through science, whose theories have no use for divine meaning and purpose. If, as Heidegger argues, a work of art both establishes and exemplifies a way things matter, that way may itself no longer matter to anyone. A work of art may cease to gather in any active sense. It may be abandoned, fall into disuse, be neglected, vandalized or otherwise disowned (treated, for example, as a mere 'museum piece', a relic of a bygone era), and such occurrences are symptomatic of the decline of the world corresponding to that work. Though a work of art founds a world, the two are nonetheless reciprocally related, mutually dependent on one another for their continuance.

In keeping with the idea of works of art as *formed* matter, as precisely *works*, Heidegger emphasizes the 'created' character of works of art. He does so, however, without placing any special weight on the person and personality of the creator. Any idea of the artist-as-singular-genius is markedly absent from his aesthetics. Indeed, he goes so far as to say at one point that 'precisely where the artist and the process and circumstances of the work's coming into being remain unknown, this thrust, this "*that*" of createdness, steps into view at its purest from out of the work' (OBT, p. 39). Heidegger does acknowledge the created character of works of art, and so the need for creators (i.e. artists), but in the light of the lately noted vulnerability of the work of art (along with the world it founds), he is equally emphatic concerning the vital role played by *preservers*: 'Just as a work cannot be without being created, just as it stands in essential need of creators, so what is created cannot come into being without preservers' (OBT, p. 40). By 'preserver' Heidegger does not mean the various specialists who dedicate themselves to the physical preservation and restoration of works of art, but rather ones who 'respond to the truth happening in the work' (OBT, p. 41). Truth in 'The Origin of the Work of Art' means 'unconcealment', which accords with the idea of ontological truth as 'disclosedness' put forward in *Being and Time*. The idea of truth-as-unconcealment is naturally paired to the notions of opening and the open that Heidegger ascribes to works of art: by opening up a world, a work of art thereby releases things from their concealment, rendering them unconcealed, open to view, but in a particular way (there is no opening onto beings as such, no 'view from nowhere', to borrow Thomas Nagel's phrase). But that unconcealment amounts to nothing if there is no one to and for whom things are so revealed, nobody who abides by that way of understanding what there is. Without preservers, a work of art is transformed into a *relic*, whose truth is now but a dead letter.

9F FURTHER PATHWAYS

'The Origin of the Work of Art' is a rich and difficult text, and we have only considered some of the main lines of thought pursued in this essay, with an eye throughout to situating this work as both a continuation of, and departure from, Heidegger's project in *Being and Time*. Before moving on to other writings from Heidegger's later philosophy, I would also like to situate the essay prospectively, in order to indicate how Heidegger's thinking continues on from this essay. Several of the ideas we have explored – the notion of a thing, the concept of earth, the importance of 'letting beings be' – are ones to which Heidegger returns repeatedly throughout his later philosophy, and to which we will return. I have also indicated at several places that 'The Origin of the Work of Art' marks the beginnings of Heidegger's thinking about *technology* – our current technological understanding of being – and the dangers he associates with its growing dominance in our lives. Heidegger's thoughts about technology are linked to his ideas about science, many of which first appear in *Being and Time*, but which change considerably in light of his growing preoccupation with technology.

There is, however, another important theme in Heidegger's later philosophy to which we have thus far paid scant attention, but whose beginnings are to be found in 'The Origins of the Work of Art'. That theme is *language*. Further reflection on some of the ideas we *have* considered, however, makes it unsurprising that Heidegger would find it important to devote considerable attention to language. Consider, for example, Heidegger's central claim that a work of art is 'the setting-itself-to-work of the truth of beings'. Truth is principally a linguistic notion, a feature of what is *said*, where what is truthfully said brings something into view, into the open (recall Heidegger's discussion of assertoric truth in *Being and Time*, where the truthful assertion points out how things are). Thus, at the heart of Heidegger's aesthetics are notions whose most natural place is within language and Heidegger by no means shies away from this appearance. On the contrary, at several points in the essay, he emphasizes it, as in the following:

> Language, by naming beings for the first time, first brings beings to word and to appearance. This naming nominates beings *to* their being and *from out of* that being. Such saying is a projecting of the clearing in which announcement is made as to what beings will come into the open as. (OBT, p. 46)

Notice how in this passage Heidegger ascribes to language much of the work he had accorded to works of art. Not surprisingly, perhaps, he asserts shortly thereafter: 'The essence of art is poetry' (OBT, p. 47). As poetic, all art thus turns out to be fundamentally (or perhaps primordially) linguistic, and so even in this essay, language turns out to be central, even fundamental.

CHAPTER 10

SCIENCE AND TECHNOLOGY

'The Origin of the Work of Art' introduces one of the central ideas of Heidegger's later philosophy, namely, the idea that what he calls 'the truth of beings' has a *history*: over the course of Western history, the truth of beings has changed in accordance with the opening and closing of different historical worlds. While 'The Origin of the Work of Art' discusses this history largely in terms of historical examples – the world of the Greek temple and the world of the Medieval cathedral – Heidegger alludes at several points to what he takes the modern truth of beings to be. He says, for example, that with the advent of the modern age, 'Beings became transparent objects capable of being mastered by calculation' (OBT, p. 48). Heidegger's appeal here to calculation and control suggests that what is definitive of the modern age is the rise of scientific thinking. Moreover, though not the central theme of his essay, Heidegger already here links the rise of this kind of thinking to a kind of loss. As 'mastered', objects are 'transparent', seen through, which suggests that something about them is ignored or overlooked (just what that is, according to Heidegger, requires considerable care in articulating).

At another point in the essay, Heidegger contrasts how a work of art 'sets forth the earth' with the way scientific inquiry ultimately destroys whatever is earthy in what it encounters. Calculating and measuring – analysis in general – serve only to destroy the materiality of what is encountered when that 'materiality' is understood in the way Heidegger associates with earth. The earthy characteristics of what is encountered go missing as soon as we approach them in calculative terms. What Heidegger refers to as 'the technological-scientific objectification of nature', which often has the 'appearance of mastery and progress', is instead 'an impotence of the will' (OBT,

p. 25) that only serves to efface what it seeks to comprehend. We can thus see in 'The Origin of the Work of Art' some indications of themes that will become central in essays written in the decades following its composition: the impact of the rise of scientific and technological thinking, both on human existence and the kind of world we encounter and engage. On the whole, Heidegger's later philosophy of science and technology can in part be understood as an attempt to measure the losses incurred by what are typically (and understandably) considered the impressive achievements in those domains. The history of the sciences and technology since the advent of modern science in the sixteenth and seventeeth centuries is apt to appear throughout as one of unalloyed *progress*, a steady increase in the scope and power of scientific theories and the correlative development of associated technologies. While Heidegger does not aim to deny such appearances outright, there is in his philosophy an attempt at least to disrupt those appearances, to suggest that something is threatened, if not lost, in the course of those gains. (The threat or 'danger' Heidegger aims to bring out is different from many of the usual ones concerning the negative impact of scientific and technological development such as the threat of nuclear annihilation, global warming, the loss of 'natural' environments and so on. It is an interesting and difficult question how Heidegger's engagement with science and technology itself engages these other, more familiar concerns. I will suggest below that the engagement is rather oblique, which should not be surprising given how rarely Heidegger treats familiar issues and concerns in a straightforward manner!)

10A SCIENCE AND THE ANNIHILATION OF THINGS

Heidegger's essay entitled 'The Thing' is throughout a meditation on loss, a kind of requiem for the proximity to *things* destroyed, paradoxically, by 'the frantic abolition of all distances' (PLT, p. 165). Though we are able to move from one place to another more quickly than ever before, and 'connect' with other parts of the world in ways and at speeds that Heidegger writing in the 1940s and 1950s could not have imagined, Heidegger argues that the net effect of all this moving and connecting is a kind of detachment, an inattention to important aspects or features of what surrounds us. Lost, in particular, is any engagement with the mere thing *as* a thing. (Here we see a place where Heidegger returns to his consideration of the notion of a thing, which served as a starting point for working out what a work of art is in 'The Origin of the Work of Art'.) But how does Heidegger come to understand the notion of a thing in the essays subsequent to 'The Origin of the Work of Art'? Moreover, how is it that things are effaced by 'technical-scientific objectivation', and why does it matter whether or not that effacement occurs? Let us take these questions more or less in order. Heidegger's account of the thing proceeds primarily by means of examples (the jug in 'The Thing', the bridge in 'Building, Dwelling, Thinking'). In attending to the jug, Heidegger emphasizes the difference between the jug, understood as a thing, and an *object*. He characterizes the jug as 'self-sustained', as 'self-supporting', and 'independent'. An object, by contrast, is to be understood primarily in relation to our experience, as something which stands 'over against' us, 'whether in immediate perception or by bringing it to mind in a recollective re-presentation' (PLT, p. 167). The thing is not a 'represented object'; in treating the thing as something primarily presented and represented, its thingly character is effaced. We can see in the contrast Heidegger draws between things and objects how he develops his earlier critique of standard accounts of a thing, those conceptions that he claimed ultimately do 'violence' to the thing. Here, he rejects the idea that being a thing consists in 'being a represented object', as that would mean defining the thing (its nature and existence) entirely in relation to our experience of it. Defining the thing this way would fail to do justice to its 'self-supporting' or 'independent' character. There is a deeper echo in this passage as well: Heidegger's talk here of the thing becoming an object when 'we place it before us' is reminiscent of his discussion in *Being and Time* of the transformation of the hammer from something useful to something objectively present when contemplation takes the place of active using. Just as the equipmental character of the item of equipment is effaced in the act of contemplation, so too is the thingly character of the thing obscured by an objectifying representation: '[N]o representation of what is present, in the sense of what stands forth and of what stands over against as an object, ever reaches to the thing *qua* thing' (PLT, pp. 168–9). And just as the hammer reveals itself most authentically when we take hold of it and hammer, so too the thingly character of the jug is revealed in its use: 'The jug's thingness resides in its being *qua* vessel. We become aware of the vessel's holding nature when we fill the jug' (PLT, p. 169).

In *Being and Time*, the revelation of what is objectively present effected by the change over from active use to detached contemplation marks the beginnings of scientific inquiry. Science recontextualizes the decontextualized *objects* discovered through contemplation, incorporating them into a systematic theory. Not surprisingly, in 'The Thing', Heidegger's contrasting of the thing with the (represented) object, though first spelled out in terms of perception and memory, quickly leads to a consideration of science. In working toward an adequate understanding of the jug *qua* thing, Heidegger first calls attention to the jug's being a vessel. Understanding the jug as a vessel leads in turn to an understanding of the jug as a *void*: in making the jug, the potter 'shapes the void'. 'From start to finish the potter takes hold of the impalpable void and brings it forth as the container in the shape of a containing vessel' (PLT, p. 169). The specific thingliness of the jug is not primarily a matter of the material which composes it, but the void the material encloses, since it is in terms of this void that its being a vessel to be filled and emptied is to be understood. It is at this point that Heidegger allows the voice of science to intrude, first by questioning this notion of a void: 'And yet, is the jug really empty?' (PLT, p. 169). The appearance of 'really' here marks an insistence that Heidegger will further develop, namely, that the sciences, physics in particular, will tell us the true nature of the thing. Heidegger writes:

> Physical science assures us that the jug is filled with air and with everything that goes to make up the air's mixture. We allowed ourselves to be misled by a semipoetic way of looking at things when we pointed to the void of the jug in order to define its acting as a container. (PLT, p. 169)

The natural sciences are here presented as offering a kind of rebuke to Heidegger's talk of the jug in terms of a shaped void, to the effect that such talk is expressive of (merely) a 'semipoetic way of looking at things'. As semipoetic, such language has no place within the natural sciences; indeed, one of the goals of science is to replace such colourful though inaccurate language with a rigorous, precise accounting of what there (really) is. Heidegger thus depicts the natural sciences as more than a little impatient with his way of talking, but Heidegger, for his part, is similarly impatient. While acknowledging the legitimacy of scientific description, at the same time he declares such descriptions incapable of reaching the thing *as* thing:

> These statements of physics are correct. By means of them, science represents something real, by which it is objectively controlled. But – is this reality the jug? No. Science always encounters only what *its* kind of representation has admitted beforehand as an object possible for science. (PLT, p. 170)

Here we see an echo of the remark from 'The Origin of the Work of Art', to the effect that the quest for objective control marks the effacement of the thing. Heidegger goes on to say that 'science makes the jug-thing a nonentity in not permitting things to be the standard for what is real' (PLT, p. 170) and, more dramatically, that 'science's knowledge, which is compelling within its own sphere, the sphere of objects, already had annihilated things as things long before the atom bomb exploded' (PLT, p. 170).

In what way does science 'annihilate' the thing? A clue to an answer lies in Heidegger's contention that 'science always encounters only what *its* kind of representation has admitted beforehand as an object possible for science.' We have seen already that 'its kind of representation' resists or rejects Heidegger's way of characterizing the thing as 'semipoetic', as a colourful but ultimately inaccurate way of characterizing what there really is. But what underwrites these charges of inaccuracy? Is it just that science prefers not to indulge in 'colourful' language? What is it really about such language that makes it inappropriate for science? Heidegger's remark in 'The Origin of the Work of Art' that in the modern age 'beings became objects that could be controlled and seen through by calculation' provides a clue. The rough idea is that the kind of control and calculation afforded by the natural sciences depends upon viewing what there is in ways that allow for *generalization* and *standardization*. Consider as an example Newton's law of gravitation, which posits a force of attraction between any two masses that varies in inverse proportion to the square of the distance between them. As a *law*, it is meant to be perfectly general or universal, applying to any and all massive bodies anywhere in the universe. As perfectly general or universal, the law factors out any other aspects or features something might have, and so considers what there is only with respect to mass. What matters for Newton's law is only the mass of an object: the law yields the same gravitational force for any two bodies of equivalent masses (provided they are the same distance apart). The objects in question may vary in myriad other respects, but the application of the law is insensitive to any such variation. Indeed, the law demands such insensitivity, as a law that pertained uniquely to one thing in virtue of its unique characteristics would not be much of a law (it is not at all clear that it makes sense to talk of such a formulation as a law at all). The power of Newton's law is precisely its indifference to anything but mass and distance, as this is what allows for its general applicability: given the law, one can calculate gravitational force for any two masses, which in turn facilitates predictions about how those bodies will behave.

Laws of nature are but one example of the kind of generality science seeks. Another example would be the ways in which experiments work within science to test and extend theories. The proper functioning of an experiment within science requires the rigorous imposition of standards and controls: the parameters of an experimental 'set-up' must be carefully determined, along with the materials and procedures employed, so as to ensure the accuracy and repeatability of the results (the notions of accuracy and repeatability are inseparable in this context). An experiment that yields a unique, one-time result is absolutely useless *as* an experiment, as it cannot be verified through repetition, nor can the results be extrapolated to other materials and situations. Thus, an effective experiment does not demonstrate something only about *this* particular entity or *this* particular sequence of events, but instead yields insights that can be applied to indefinitely many entities or events that satisfy the well-defined constraints maintained by the experimental set-up. (Consider as an example the testing of a new drug or medication: in testing its efficacy or safety, we don't want to know only what it does on this particular occasion with respect to this particular specimen (this lab rat, say, or this volunteer); the whole point of the test is to tell us something that extends beyond this one instance.)

Scientific practice thus requires an indifference to, indeed intolerance of, what we might call *particularity*. The ways in which science 'treats' what there is (as point-masses, material systems, molecular compounds, zoological specimens and so on) are in the service of obtaining general (or generalizable) results: laws and principles that can be applied in virtue of something's instantiating the features generalized over by the law or principle in question. Such regimentation is at odds with the kind of particularity Heidegger ascribes to the thing. Note what Heidegger says in connection with the jug:

> In the scientific view, the wine became a liquid, and liquidity in turn became one of the states of aggregation of matter, *possible everywhere*. We failed to give thought to what the jug holds and how it holds. (PLT, p. 171 – my emphasis)

Heidegger's reference to 'the states of aggregation of matter' summarizes the ways in which the sciences efface the particularity of things: physics can only recognize the jug as, at best, one aggregation of matter, predictably related to other aggregates. I say 'at best' here because the notion of an *aggregate* has a kind of vagueness built into it: aggregates are not well-defined individuals, with well-delineated boundaries, such that questions concerning where an aggregate begins and ends, where one leaves off and another starts, do not admit of precise answers. From the standpoint of physics, the jug is much like the second of the physicist Sir Arthur Eddington's celebrated 'two tables' in *The Nature of the Physical World*. What Eddington refers to as the first table is the table as ordinarily perceived and described: something solid, relatively well defined and individuated, set off from its surroundings and so, as he puts it, 'substantial'. The 'second' table is the table as described by physics: 'My scientific table is mostly emptiness. Sparsely scattered in that emptiness are numerous electric charges rushing about with great speed; but their combined bulk amounts to less than a billionth of the bulk of the table itself.' From the standpoint of physics the substantiality of the table evanesces; indeed, the table is no longer manifest as an individual entity at all, but a kind of clustering (or aggregation) of the particles distributed in a volume of space where that clustering lacks precise borders and is really mostly empty space anyway: 'There is nothing *substantial* about my second table. It is nearly all empty space – space pervaded, it is true, by fields of force, but these are assigned to the category of "influences", not of "things".' Eddington does not, of course, think that there are really two tables, but two, ultimately competing, descriptions of what there is. Much of his argument is concerned to demonstrate the superiority of the second, scientific conception of reality, and so the outmoded, almost mythological character of the first: 'The whole trend of modern scientific views is to break down the separate categories of "things", "influences", "forms", etc.' 'Break down' is not far short of 'annihilate'; either way, Eddington makes it clear that the notion of a thing, described by Heidegger as 'independent' and 'self-supporting', has no place in the language and outlook of modern science. As a result, Eddington would no doubt reproach Heidegger for his 'semipoetic' language insofar as that language is meant to convey a serious conception of reality.

In *What Is Called Thinking?*, Heidegger engages explicitly with the kind of view espoused by Eddington, when he invites us to consider (indeed, think about) standing before a tree in bloom. What Heidegger wants to keep in view via this invitation is the character of any such episode *as* an encounter with the tree, as an episode of meeting the tree 'face-to-face'. 'As we are in this relation of one to the other and before the other, the tree and we *are*' (WCT, p. 41). The principal thrust of Heidegger's discussion of this example is that much of what passes for thinking in philosophy and science falsifies such encounters, either by analysing the 'perceptual experience' of the one standing before the tree as a series of 'internal' mental (or neural) events such that the idea that the tree *is* drops out of the picture *or* by analysing the tree scientifically, which again leads to a kind of obliteration of the tree: 'Physics, physiology, and psychology . . . explain to us that what we see and accept is properly not a tree but in reality a void, thinly sprinkled with electric charges here and there that race hither and yon at enormous speeds' (WCT, p. 43). To adopt this perspective is to 'forfeit everything', since this perspective rules out the possibility of understanding this encounter as genuinely involving a 'face-to-face' meeting with a tree, which means that *anything* we are inclined to understand as a genuine engagement with 'self-supporting' things must be dismissed as a kind of quaint delusion or illusion. The important thing, for Heidegger, is to resist the allure of these modern, scientifically informed perspectives, as they are but the latest way of analysing, rather than thinking through, our untutored experience of the world. The threat posed by such analysis is the obliteration of that experience; the difficulty is still to think about it (Heidegger is *not* recommending that we just be oblivious) without such an analytical eye. As he contended in 'The Origin of the Work of Art', doing this requires letting beings be:

When we think through what this is, that tree in bloom presents itself to us so that we can come and stand face-to-face with it, the thing that matters first and foremost, and finally, is not to drop the tree in bloom, but for once to let it stand where it stands. Why do we say 'finally'? Because to this day, thought has never let the tree stand where it stands. (WCT, p. 44)

We will consider shortly what is required to let things such as the tree be what they are. Perhaps surprisingly, a great deal of it has to do with how one thinks about (and uses) language. Before that, we need to consider Heidegger's views on technology.

10B MODERN TECHNOLOGY AS CHALLENGING-FORTH

There is a long-standing tendency to think about the relation between science and technology in the following manner: science is a kind of pure, theoretical inquiry, a disinterested attempt to figure reality out, while technology is the more interested application of those pure results. On this account, science has a kind of primacy, as it supplies the research that makes technological innovation or development possible. As Heidegger sees it, this way of thinking about science and technology obscures at least as much as it reveals. For one thing, the relation between scientific theorizing and technological innovation is far more complicated than this idea of a one-way line of research followed by application. Often, theoretical development is only possible given technological achievements: various things about atoms, for example, could only be discovered once researchers had figured out ways to isolate, smash and measure them. As Heidegger notes (well before it was fashionable to emphasize this point): 'Modern physics, as experimental, is dependent upon technical apparatus and upon progress in the building of apparatus' (QCT, p. 14). While Heidegger thinks that 'the establishing of this mutual relationship between technology and physics is correct', he regards this as 'a merely historiographical establishing of facts and says nothing about that in which this mutual relationship is grounded' (QCT, p. 14). Missing from this historiography is any insight into the 'essence' or 'ground' of both modern science and technology. To ask after the essence in this context is to ask after the most general characterization of this stage in the history of being. What, in other words, is the 'truth of beings' in the modern, scientific-technological age?

In thinking about the essence of technology, we need to be careful not simply to enumerate various kinds of technologies and technological devices and try to extract some set of common features. The essence of technology 'is by no means anything technological', and so Heidegger warns that 'we shall never experience our relationship to the essence of technology so long as we merely conceive and push forward the technological, put up with it, or evade it' (QCT, p. 4). Heidegger is especially concerned that we not stop with what seems like the obvious answer to his question. This easy answer consists of two statements: 'One says: Technology is a means to an end. The other says: Technology is a human activity' (QCT, p. 4). We might think of this as the build-a-better-mousetrap conception of technology, where there are already independently defined goals or ends (such as trapping mice), and human beings try to devise better means to those ends (such as by devising more sophisticated, efficient, reliable, humane, etc. kinds of traps). Technology on this view is subservient to ends that are otherwise already in place; technology is, moreover, subservient to us, to human beings who devise machines, devices, contraptions and so on.

Heidegger allows that there is something 'correct' about this 'instrumental' and 'anthropological' conception of technology. Indeed, it seems obviously right to say that technology does in many ways serve to attain ends that can be independently specified, and it again seems obviously right that technological devices are devised by people (they certainly don't spring up like mushrooms, reproduce like animals or fall from the sky like pennies from heaven). Although there is something correct about this definition, Heidegger thinks it is at best shallow (later in the essay, Heidegger seems unwilling to allow even this much, saying instead that it is 'in principle untenable' (QCT, p. 21)). The superficiality of this definition is evident for Heidegger in its failure to think through the means–ends relation to which it appeals. What kind of relation is this? What does it mean for something to serve as, or be, an instrument? Consider the following example. We say that a guitar is a musical instrument; it is thus a means to the end of producing music. If we leave the specification of the end as simply 'producing music', then the end does appear to be independent of the means: music can be played on or with the guitar, but also myriad other instruments as well. If I want to play 'Yankee Doodle', I can just as easily plink it out on the piano as pick it out on the guitar. There is, however, something misleading in this purported independence, whose plausibility is maintained by only specifying the end in a very general way. Though we might produce *some* music in some other way – using some other instrument – the music would not be *guitar music* without being played on the guitar (we can ignore for now the issue of synthesized guitar music). The guitar, in the hands of a musician, produces or 'brings forth' a very particular kind of music, and so even though the same 'tune' can be played on different instruments, in each case there is something irreducibly different. Moreover, the musician is the *kind* of musician he is in virtue of the instrument(s) he plays: many of the skills and abilities he has cannot be easily separated from those very instruments or transferred to others (a skilled guitarist may be totally at sea with a trombone, for example). The guitarist does not simply put the guitar to use, to produce something that might be brought about in some other way. If he were to sit down at the piano instead, that would not simply be using a different means to the same end; both the musician and the end would thereby be transformed as well.

The guitar, as an instrument, produces something, brings it forth, in a way that would not otherwise be possible. Guitar music does not just naturally occur, nor does the guitar more effectively facilitate the production of something that might be produced otherwise. But even in cases where the relation between means and ends, instrument and product, is not as tight, i.e. where there is a greater degree of independence in the specification of the means and ends, this rela- tion of producing or bringing forth remains. The instrument is instrumental in bringing something forth, and so in revealing it *as* something so produced. For Heidegger, the revelatory capacity of the instrument links the instrument to the notion of *truth*, again understood as bringing things into unconcealment. He concludes from this that 'technology is therefore no mere means. Technology is a way of revealing. If we give heed to this, then another whole realm for the essence of technology will open itself up to us. It is the realm of revealing, i.e., of truth' (QCT, p. 12).

The problem with this line of thinking is that it does not (yet) differ- entiate *modern* technology from more general and long-standing phenomena. After all, human beings were producing things – using tools and instruments, deploying particular techniques and developing manufacturing procedures – well before the scientific and industrial revolutions whose advent Heidegger links to the 'annihilation' of things. Central to Heidegger's questioning of technology is that modern technology *is* a distinctive phenomenon. Thus, if the *essence* of modern technology is to be understood as a way of revealing, that 'way' must somehow stand apart from the ways in which 'traditional' technologies have been revelatory: 'What is modern technology? It too is a revealing. Only when we allow our attention to rest on this fundamental characteristic does that which is new in modern technology show itself to us' (QCT, p. 14).

Heidegger links traditional, pre-modern technologies, as bringing-forth, with *poiesis*: what is produced in these traditional technologies is brought into the open *as* distinctive, particular things. The rough idea is that hand-crafted items, for example, each have a kind of uniqueness or particularity, as each bears the traces of its own particular production, its own history. A skilled artisan is not a machine, nor does she strive to be: each item produced by the artist has its own history that is reflected in the sometimes slight, sometimes pronounced differences from the others the artisan has produced. Modern, machine technology strives precisely for the kind of uniformity that is so alien to skilled handicrafts: items that one buys 'off-the-shelf' should as much as possible be alike with one another, so that it does not matter that I choose this one rather than that one (and even when I opt for a 'custom' item, it is nonetheless customized in a standard way). But this means that the individual entity is not revealed as an individual, but instead as one of a more general kind, which can be substituted without effect more or less at will. Modern technology is not revelatory in the traditional sense, but in a wholly new way: the way of revealing characteristic of modern technology can be discerned not so much in what gets produced, the particular entities brought forth (since their particularity has been so deeply effaced), but in the underlying ways in which everything is organized so as to facilitate this kind of uniform, standardized production. Heidegger refers to this underlying way first as a kind of *challenging*: 'The revealing that rules throughout modern technology has the character of setting-upon, in the sense of a challenging-forth' (QCT, p. 16).

By 'challenging-forth', Heidegger means a view of what there is exclusively in terms what we might call *effective use*: what something is is a matter of what it can best be used for, where 'best' means most effectively or efficiently. (Machine-made goods exemplify this idea of challenging forth, since machines, with their standardized methods of production, produce items more efficiently than by hand: machines are faster and, due to the absence of variation, make fewer mistakes.) The paradigmatic example of this way of revealing, which underwrites and informs its emergence in other domains, is that of *energy*: 'The revealing that rules in modern technology is a challenging, which puts to nature the unreasonable demand that it supply energy that can be extracted and stored as such' (QCT, p. 14). In energy production, the earth is 'challenged' in various ways – oil wells are drilled; coal seams are mined; atoms are split; rivers are dammed – to yield energy, which can then in turn be used to power automobiles, factories, railway systems, airplanes and so on, and these too are subject to this challenging. Factories are challenged to produce the greatest amount at the least cost (where cost might be measured in various ways); railway systems are challenged to deliver goods (the faster and cheaper the better); automobiles are challenged to carry drivers and passengers effectively (where that might be a matter of speed, comfort, smoothness of ride and so on). According to this modern technological way of revealing:

> Everywhere everything is ordered to stand by, to be immediately at hand, indeed to stand there just so that it may be on call for a further ordering. Whatever is ordered about in this way has its own standing. We call it the standing-reserve. (QCT, p. 17)

What is translated as 'standing-reserve' (the German is *Bestand*) might be more straightforwardly rendered as simply *resource*: to challenge-forth means to reveal what there is as a variety of resources, to be effectively organized and used. We should be careful here not to construe this notion of world-as-resource as applying only within straightforwardly industrial contexts. Though abundantly evident in power plants and factories, the understanding of being that underwrites modern technological culture is far more, indeed maximally, pervasive. Even those things that might be regarded as escapes from the pressures of industrialized society – vacations, communing with nature, leisure time – are themselves resources to be challenged: my vacation is challenged to yield comfort and relaxation, my walk in the woods edification, while my 'leisure time' is itself a resource to be used effectively.

A careful reader might well at this point wonder how Heidegger's observations concerning the way a technological understanding of being reveals what there is as a network of resources square with his earlier characterization of Da-sein's world as a referential total-ity of useful entities. As we saw in our discussion of his introduction of the notion of *earth* in 'The Origin of the Work of Art', Heidegger in *Being and Time* does not allow for anything in everydayness that resists the category of handiness apart from the mere stuff of object-ive presence, which, as amenable to scientific theorizing, lacks the 'revealing-concealing' character of his later notion of earth. For everyday Da-sein, 'The forest is a forest of timber, the mountain a quarry of rock, the river is water power, the wind is wind "in the sails"' (BT, p. 66/69). This does not sound too far off from the idea of resource or standing-reserve as it appears in 'The Question Concerning Technology', though in *Being and Time* Heidegger's descriptions are not cast in any kind of negative light: that everyday Da-sein encounters things in this manner does not seem to be any cause for concern or worry. But the technological understanding of being is something that Heidegger regards as an 'extreme danger'. There are no such alarms being sounded in *Being and Time*.

The question arises of whether this new tone of alarm marks another example of the divergence between early and later Heidegger. In other words, is Heidegger in 'The Question Concern-ing Technology' casting his earlier descriptions of everyday experi-ence in a darker, more worrisome way? There seems to me to be two ways of handling these sorts of questions. One way is to see Heidegger's descriptions in *Being and Time* as at least intimating what he will later describe as the technological mode of revealing, and so we can understand Heidegger in his later essays to be delving deeper into phenomena already in view in *Being and Time*. This way makes a certain degree of sense, since what Heidegger later describes as the essence of technology would already have held sway in the era in which he is writing *Being and Time*. Thus, a descriptively adequate account of everyday Da-sein should carry traces at least of this tech-nological way of revealing, even without being named as such and even without being painted in dark or ominous tones. That Heidegger so paints it later is evidence of further reflection on more or less the same phenomena: that everyday Da-sein sees a forest as 'a forest of timber' or the mountain as 'a quarry of rock' is some-thing that later struck Heidegger as symptomatic of a deeply dis-turbing, threatening way of revealing what there is.

There is, however, another interpretive move one could make, which does not postulate this kind of continuity between *Being and*

Time and the later writings on technology. According to this approach, the descriptions Heidegger offers in *Being and Time* are meant to be far more general, and so in a sense more neutral, than what he later describes under the rubric of the essence of technology. Encountering things as useful is not equivalent to encountering what there is as standing-reserve, since one can do the former without doing the latter. After all, everyday Da-sein is not a creature specifically of modernity, and so the idea that Da-sein encounters things as useful or handy should likewise not be so confined: premodern, everyday Da-sein encounters what there is as useful, though not as resources in the modern, technological sense. There are passages in 'The Question Concerning Technology' that make this kind of distinction. Most notably, immediately after introducing the idea of 'challenging', with its demands on nature to 'supply energy that can be extracted and stored as such', he asks:

> But does this not hold for the old windmill as well? No. Its sails do indeed turn in the wind; they are left entirely to the wind's blowing. But the windmill does not unlock energy from the air currents in order to store it. (QCT, p. 14)

Heidegger's choice of a windmill is especially apt, as it harkens back to his descriptions in *Being and Time* without explicitly referring to them. The owner of the windmill no doubt encounters the wind as 'wind in the sails', but Heidegger's suggestion is that this is not (yet) the kind of challenging-forth characteristic of modern technology. (I leave aside whether Heidegger can sustain this distinction; what matters for now is just that he wants to make it at all.) This example is followed closely by another, which contrasts the field worked by the peasant and one cultivated by 'the mechanized food industry':

> The field that the peasant formerly cultivated and set in order appears differently than it did when to set in order still meant to take care of and to maintain. The work of the peasant does not challenge the soil of the field. In the sowing of the grain it places the seed in the keeping of the forces of growth and watches over its increase. But meanwhile even the cultivation of the field has come under the grip of another kind of setting-in-order, which *sets* upon nature. It sets upon it in the sense of challenging it. Agriculture is now the mechanized food industry. (QCT, pp. 14–15)

Finally, Heidegger mentions 'the forester who, in the wood, measures the felled timber and to all appearances walks the same forest path in the same way as did his grandfather'; despite the apparent similarity between the forester today and his grandfather, he is 'today commanded by profit-making in the lumber industry, whether he knows it or not' (QCT, p. 18). In all these contrasting cases, it seems clear that the category of useful things is equally applicable to both sides of the contrast – the forester's grandfather certainly experienced his trusty axe as something *for* felling trees, the peasant his plough as something *for* tilling the fields and so on – though not the notion of standing-reserve. Again, Heidegger's insistence here on this distinction may not be well founded, as there may be more than a little dewy-eyed nostalgia for bygone times in his characterizations of pre-modern life (I will try to address this charge of nostalgia below). Be that as it may, it is nonetheless significant that Heidegger does so insist, which suggests that we should be extremely cautious in any attempt to assimilate handiness (or readiness-to-hand) and standing-reserve.

10C TECHNOLOGY AS ENFRAMING

The notions of challenging-forth and standing-reserve are bound together by a third term: 'We now name that challenging claim which gathers man thither to order the self-revealing as standing-reserve: "*Ge-stell*" [Enframing]' (QCT, p. 19). As Heidegger himself acknowledges, he is here deploying an ordinary German word to do some extraordinary work: 'According to ordinary usage, the word *Gestell* means some kind of apparatus, e.g., a book rack. *Gestell* is also the name for a skeleton' (QCT, p. 20). My German–English dictionary also lists 'stand', 'rack', 'chassis' and 'bedstead' among the meanings for *Gestell*. Varying only by the addition of a hyphen, 'the employment of the word *Ge-stell* that is now required of us seems equally eerie [as using it as the name for a skeleton], not to speak of the arbitrariness with which words of a mature language are thus misused' (QCT, p. 20). Despite his own admissions of idiosyncrasy, Heidegger's terminology here is not overly difficult to understand (at least no more so than other ordinary and coined terms he puts to his own philosophical uses), as it serves to summarize the driving idea of modern technology of ordering what there is as standing-reserve. *Ge-stell* is more naturally translated as 'framework', which easily allows the insertion of a hyphen ('frame-work'). *Ge-stell* thus suggests working over what there is, working it into one all-encompassing framework, i.e. ordering what there is as an interconnected system of resources to be exploited in order to yield resources that themselves can be ordered: 'In Enframing, that unconcealment comes to pass in conformity with which the work of modern technology reveals the real as standing-reserve. This work is therefore neither only a human activity nor a mere means within such activity' (QCT, p. 21).

Heidegger's last remark further illustrates the limitations of the anthropological, instrumental conception of technology canvassed at the opening of the essay. Indeed, the conception is doubly problematic, foundering both with respect to instrumentality and anthropology. To begin with the former, if Heidegger is right about the distinctive character of technological revealing, as the ordering of what there is as a framework of resources, then it is not merely instrumental with respect to already-defined ends or goals. Technology, as a distinctive mode of revealing, is transformative not just with respect to means, but to ends as well. More radically, there is ultimately something distinctly endless about modern technology, which is driven by a demand for effective, efficient ordering, which leads only to more ordering and so on. In the end, efficiency becomes a kind of endless end-in-itself. Moreover, the demand for efficient ordering is not simply something that human beings do or make; human beings are no less subject to the challenging-forth characteristic of modern technology: 'Enframing means the gathering together of that setting-upon which sets upon man, i.e., challenges him forth, to reveal the real, in the mode of ordering, as standing-reserve' (QCT, p. 20). This is why Heidegger ultimately concludes that 'the merely instrumental, merely anthropological definition of technology is therefore in principle untenable' (QCT, p. 21).

10D THE 'SUPREME DANGER' OF MODERN TECHNOLOGY

The idea that man himself is as much set-upon by modern technology as anything else is very much at odds with a standard conception of technology, wherein it constitutes the epitome of human domination or mastery. On this standard model, human beings utilize technology to further their own various ends (here we see how the instrumental and anthropological conceptions of technology fit together). Heidegger acknowledges that there is something right about this: 'Who accomplishes the challenging setting-upon through which what we call the real is revealed as standing-reserve? Obviously, man. To what extent is man capable of such a revealing? Man can indeed conceive, fashion, and carry through this or that in one way or another' (QCT, p. 18). Correct though these answers are, there is ultimately something deeply misleading about them, and in two respects. The first respect concerns the relation that obtains generally between the different understandings of being that have arisen and declined over time and human beings, in that these various understandings, their arising and declining, are not themselves human achievements or accomplishments. The ways in which beings are revealed are not subject to human control. That is why Heidegger follows up his pair of questions and answers with the qualification that 'man does not have control over unconcealment itself, in which at any given time the real shows itself or withdraws. The fact that the real has been showing itself in the light of Ideas ever since the time of Plato, Plato did not bring about. The thinker only responded to what addressed itself to him' (QCT, p. 18). Here we can see a development of Heidegger's appeal to *thrownness* in *Being and Time*, which named the way in which Da-sein is 'delivered over' to its existence. Da-sein cannot get back behind its thrownness and achieve a kind of self-mastery all the way down (Da-sein, as authentic or self-owned, can only resolutely take over its already ongoing projection of possibilities).

Human beings are the ones for whom, in a space of intelligibility afforded by the opening of a clearing, things are manifest or intelligible, but the shape of that space so to speak is not itself something that human beings control; rather, the shape is something to which human beings are 'destined'. Any such way of being destined involves what Heidegger refers to as 'danger': 'The destining of revealing is as such, in every one of its modes, and therefore necessarily, *danger*' (QCT, p. 26). The danger lies in the ways in which every way of revealing is also a concealing: one way of opening onto what there is is at the same time a closing off of another way. Heidegger suggests, for example, that the rise of a cause–effect understanding of reality closes off an understanding of God as something mysterious and holy: God is reduced to 'the god of the philosophers', the first in an order of efficient causes.

What might have originally seemed exalted, a testimony to God's supremacy, is now either only a kind of causal supremacy or sentimental superstition.

Thus, the human-beings-as-masters picture is at odds with what holds generally with respect to revealing and concealing, but the rise of modern technology further disrupts this picture despite its tendency to lend credence to that very idea. Heidegger claims that 'when destining reigns in the mode of Enframing, it is the supreme danger'. (QCT, p. 26). Heidegger says that this heightened, indeed 'supreme', danger 'attests itself in two ways'. The first is the kind of disappearance or annihilation already noted in our discussion of the fate of *things* in scientific theorizing. However, in 'The Question Concerning Technology', Heidegger extends this sense of disappearance all the way to *objects*; 'thing' and 'object' are by no means equivalent notions for the later Heidegger, and so it is not at all clear that we can identify *this* disappearance with the one worked out in such essays as 'The Thing' and 'Building, Dwelling, Thinking'. At the same time, the proximity of the initial laying out of these ideas in his Bremen lectures suggests a close relation. Scientific theorizing and practice efface the particularity of things by demanding repeatability and generalizability, but this demand is itself subservient to the kind of challenging-forth central to technology. Calculability, predictability, standardization, generalizability, all such notions ultimately contribute to the effective and efficient exploitation of the world as a vast system of resources. Human beings thereby find themselves 'in the midst of objectlessness', and so as 'nothing but the orderer of the standing-reserve'. The first attestation to the 'supreme danger' of enframing precipitates the second: since technology relegates to human beings the sole task of being the 'orderer of the standing-reserve', this brings them to 'the very brink of a precipitous fall'. The 'fall' in question involves human beings ultimately being subjected to enframing, that is, coming to view themselves as just more standing-reserve.

The supreme danger is thus one of human beings becoming just more resources to be effectively and efficiently ordered. Heidegger himself notes the advent of the phrase 'human resources', which is by now well entrenched in common usage, but again it is important not to limit the phenomena he is describing to specifically work-related contexts. While it may be true that the workplace is one place where the transformation of human beings into resources is especially evident, it is by no means the only place. Consider, for example, another common conception of human beings in modern society, namely as *consumers*. As the name suggests, consumers are users of resources, which by itself establishes a connection with standing-reserve. But the designation also pulls human beings within the sphere in another way: consumers do not just use resources, but are themselves resources to be measured, quantified and indexed. Consumers collectively form *markets* for goods and services, and those purveying such goods and services strategize endlessly to target those markets effectively. Witness the almost-constant deluge of advertising on everything from television to T-shirts, websites to stickers on fruit. While those ads may offer the appearance of addressing a 'unique you', an 'individual', they are very much aimed at an anonymous, multiple audience, whose 'value' is measured in 'spending power' (hence, some collectives of consumers are more valuable resources than others, as the frenzied quest for 'reaching' the 18–34 year-old market illustrates). But being a consumer is not just a way of being designated, from the outside, but it is an attitude or orientation that one can take up and inhabit. That is, consuming is a way of being, a way of organizing my activities, such that 'What can I buy today?' becomes an all-important question (leading a life dominated by consumption can be far more subtle than this, in the sense that living primarily as a consumer need not involve ever explicitly asking this question of oneself).

Being a consumer is one way of being a resource, but certainly not the only way (Heidegger at one point mentions being a patient, understood as part of a 'supply' for a clinic, which seems in these HMO-dominated days to be all the more relevant). We might see Heidegger's worries about the threat of human beings becoming resources as taking over the role occupied by *das Man* in *Being and Time*, as again part of the threat concerns similar kinds of anonymity and interchangeability. Moreover, there are similarities with respect to what specifically is threatened in each case. Recall that the threat posed by *das Man* resides in the ways in which it conceals, indeed actively suppresses especially when it comes to death, the idea that Da-sein's being is an issue for it. Da-sein, as a *Man*-self, fails to face up to the kind of being it is, and so fails to take over its being as something whose projection it is responsible for. The threat posed by the transformation of human beings into resources is similar in the sense that it likewise obscures from view something essential about human beings: 'The rule of Enframing threatens man with the possibility that it could be denied to him to enter into a more original revealing and hence to experience the call of a more primal truth' (QCT, p. 28).

Enframing 'conceals revealing itself' (QCT, p. 27), which would appear to mean that the technological way of things showing up does not itself show up *as* a way of showing up (Heidegger suggests this meaning when he says that 'man stands so decisively in attendance on the challenging-forth of Enframing that he does not apprehend Enframing as a claim' (QCT, p. 27)). Rather, it shows up as something for which no competitor or alternative ways of showing up are possible. Once everything is enframed as a resource, then there are simply more or less efficient ways of 'ordering' those resources. For example, where I live in West Virginia, coal is still an abundant natural resource, but many environmentalists have tried to argue that in the long term, areas unmarred by coal mining are more valuable for tourism and recreation. On the face of it, the anti-mining side of the argument wishes to halt the challenging-forth of West Virginia's landscape. But notice that the argument here is framed in terms of resources on *both* sides: what is at issue in the debate is what kind of resource something is best understood as being (a resource for energy production versus a resource for tourism and recreation), where 'best' means most effectively used overall. The idea that West Virginia's undeveloped areas are something *other* than resources – places of intrinsic value, say, or 'sacred space' – is apt to be met with a smile of derision as a kind of quaint, 'crunchy' outlook founded more on sentiment than any kind of rationality. While this might be part of what Heidegger has in mind, the idea that technological revealing broaches no alternatives cannot be the whole of the matter, since he has already said that *every* historical understanding of being – every opening onto what there is – carries the danger of concealing alternative ways of things being revealed. The Medieval Christian understanding of being did not exactly countenance alternatives either, nor did the world of the Greek temple: for those who inhabited those worlds, those worlds did not have the status of one way things show up among others. That enframing 'conceals revealing itself' must mean something more than that the 'reach' of enframing promises to be total (again, Medieval Christianity aspired to that kind of reach too).

What Heidegger has in mind here in explaining the 'supreme danger' of modern technology is not so much whether that understanding countenances alternatives, but whether human beings, as themselves enframed, can any longer be receptive to alternatives. All of the previous epochs in the history of being have clearly allowed for, though perhaps did not necessarily encourage, that kind of receptivity, since new openings onto what there is came to replace them. This is a deeper kind of threat than the danger that is part and parcel of any historical understanding of being, since it threatens to alter the 'essence' of human beings (notice also that the threat is other than the standard litany of threats cited in relation to technological development):

> The threat to man does not come in the first instance from the potentially lethal machines and apparatus of technology. The actual threat has already affected man in his essence. The rule of Enframing threatens man with the possibility that it could be denied to him to enter into a more original revealing and hence to experience the call of a more primal truth. (QCT, p. 28)

As one more resource among others, to be ordered effectively and efficiently, human beings may no longer be able to view themselves in a distinctive way, as the ones to and for whom things are disclosed. Because enframing encompasses human beings in the same way as everything else, 'man . . . fails in every way to hear in what respect he ek-sists, from out of his essence, in the realm of an exhortation or address, and thus *can never* encounter only himself' (QCT, p. 27). Again, there is an echo of *Being and Time* here. Just as the danger Heidegger warns of bears traces of the ways the conformity demanded by *das Man* blocks Da-sein's insight into the special character of its own existence, the importance noted here of man encountering 'only himself' is reminiscent of the *anxiety* that 'individualizes' Da-sein, thereby breaking the grip of *das Man*. Using the terminology of *Being and Time*, Heidegger's concern here is that Da-sein may no longer have the capacity for anxiety, and so may no longer experience itself in a distinctive way. (What might have previously counted as anxiety may be just one more thing to be effectively managed.)

10E THE SAVING POWER

Despite the darkness of Heidegger's tone in 'The Question Concerning Technology' (and elsewhere in his later writings), his attitude is not exclusively pessimistic. Despite the 'extreme danger' posed by the advent of the modern technological age, there remains the possibility of developing what he calls at the outset of the essay a 'free relationship' to technology. He explains that 'the relationship will be free if it opens our human existence to the essence of technology' (QCT, p. 3). By the close of the essay, Heidegger further develops this idea, noting that, paradoxically, the possibility of such a 'free relationship' is bound up with the notion of enframing:

> It is precisely in Enframing, which threatens to sweep man away into ordering as the supposed single way of revealing, and so thrusts man into the danger of the surrender of his free essence – it is precisely in this extreme danger that the innermost indestructible belongingness of man within granting may come to light, provided that we, for our part, begin to pay heed to the coming to presence of technology. (QCT, p. 32)

Heidegger presents his thinking here as guided by the words of the poet Hölderlin, who writes:

> *But where danger is, grows*
> *The saving power also.*

The 'saving power' is not so much technology, or even enframing, itself (as when people talk about technological solutions to the problems engendered by the spread of technology), but what Heidegger here calls 'paying heed' to technology. The idea here is that the very activity of questioning the essence of technology, of revealing enframing as that essence, is constitutive of remaining free with respect to technology, since that activity (thinking) is constitutive of human freedom in general. By thinking in this manner, we are thereby

> sojourning within the open space of destining, a destining that in no way confines us to a stultified compulsion to push on blindly with technology or, what comes to the same thing, to rebel

helplessly against it and curse it as the work of the devil. Quite to the contrary, when we once open ourselves expressly to the *essence* of technology, we find ourselves unexpectedly taken into a freeing claim. (QCT, pp. 25–6)

Developing a free relationship to technology does not mean aspiring to a life free *from* technology (though Heidegger's nostalgia for the life of pre-technological peasants sometimes encourages this interpretation), but instead leading a life that is not pervasively ordered by technology. In his address '*Gelassenheit*', translated as 'Discourse on Thinking' (but meaning something like 'releasement' or 'letting-be-ness'), Heidegger spells out this notion of a free relation in remarkably straightforward terms:

We can use technical devices, and yet with proper use also keep ourselves so free of them, that we may let go of them at any time. We can use technical devices as they ought to be used, and also let them alone as something which does not affect our inner and real core. We can affirm the unavoidable use of technical devices, and also deny them the right to dominate us, and so to warp, confuse, and lay waste our nature. (DT, p. 54)

If we can succeed in maintaining this orientation to technology, 'our relation to technology will become wonderfully simple and relaxed. We let technical devices enter into our daily life, and at the same time leave them outside, that is, let them alone, as things which are nothing absolute but remain dependent upon something higher' (DT, p. 54).

It is not entirely clear what this 'wonderfully simple and relaxed' relation to technology is really supposed to look like, nor is it clear how one really sets about developing or maintaining such a relation. Various ideas suggest themselves – turning off the television; leaving one's cellular phone off (or, better, at home); spending less time on the computer; recognizing alternative ways to get from one place to another – but it is uncertain whether these sorts of helpful hints are what Heidegger has in mind and, if they are, whether they cut deep enough to establish the kind of free relation he has in mind. (All of the ones I have proposed may not cut deep enough by all being *individual* in nature, whereas the kind of enframing Heidegger warns of operates much more globally.) It may, however, be enough that such small endeavours start one on the way toward the kind of relationship he is naming here. By striving to make 'technical devices' count less – for example, by no longer frantically checking one's voicemail or e-mail, by no longer organizing one's time according to what programmes are on television, by getting out and walking rather than always driving everywhere – doing these things mark a refusal to *bind oneself* to technology; doing that, in turn, facilitates the recognition that insofar as one is, or has been, bound to technology, that is something one *can* undo (or at least alleviate), and recognizing *that* just is the recognition of one's own freedom in relation to the technological. Heidegger says that 'everything, then, depends upon this: that we ponder this arising and that, recollecting, we watch over it' (QCT, p. 32). The small steps enumerated here, though neither complete nor decisive, at least serve to foster the kind of pondering and recollecting he calls for, as each of them involves (and encourages) a kind of mindfulness with respect to technology. The 'simple and relaxed' relation Heidegger describes, wherein one is not dominated by technology, involves a continued willingness to think about one's relation to the myriad 'technical devices' that populate our lives, and that kind of thinking is a step, at least, on the way to the deeper level of thought Heidegger himself enacts in 'The Question Concerning Technology'.

But all of this can never entirely counteract the danger posed by the advent of technology: 'Human activity can never directly counter this danger. Human achievement alone can never banish it. But human reflection can ponder the fact that all saving power must be of a higher essence than what is endangered, though at the same time kindred to it' (QCT, pp. 33–4). There appears to be a residual pessimism in Heidegger's writing after all, insofar as he discourages the idea that some concrete course of action might cure what ails us in the modern age. The best one can do is to continue to question – 'For questioning is the piety of thought' (QCT, p. 35) – and this means questioning the ways in which science and technology encourage us to conceive of and describe the world (including ourselves). Recall the ways in which science dismisses more poetic modes of speech, which amounts to a dismissal of the things named and called to by that speech. At the close of 'The Question Concerning Technology', Heidegger again invokes Hölderlin in order to suggest that the 'saving power' he envisions resides nowhere else than in the poetic dimensions of language:

The same poet from whom we heard the words

But where danger is, grows
The saving power also.

says to us:

. . . *poetically dwells man upon this earth.* (QCT, p. 34)

To Heidegger's thoughts on poetry and dwelling we now turn.

CHAPTER 11

LANGUAGE, DWELLING AND THE FOURFOLD

Heidegger's invocation of Hölderlin's phrase '. . . poetically man dwells . . .' at the close of 'The Question Concerning Technology' is by no means a singular moment in his later philosophy. The phrase also serves as the title of another essay (see PLT, pp. 213–29) and more generally, it names ideas that Heidegger ponders and strives to articulate in large stretches of his later philosophy. We can make considerable headway in understanding his later philosophy if we follow some of those attempts to locate the special significance of the *poetic* and its relation to the idea of *dwelling*. Each of these is central to his efforts to spell out the 'extreme danger' posed by the technological understanding of being, as well as the 'saving power' that resides in the attempt to make that essence manifest. Very roughly, the technological and scientific understanding of being that has come to dominate modern human life threatens the possibility of dwelling. Saying just this much indicates that by 'dwelling' Heidegger means something more than simply existing, being alive and so forth; instead, he uses 'dwelling' as a way of expressing the conditions of what Heidegger takes to be a fully human life. That a fully human life is *conditioned* is part of what technology tends to obscure: since everything shows up as a resource to be exploited, what there is is subject to human desires and demands, while those demands and desires are not themselves subject to anything (here we see again how technology fosters the man-as-master illusion).

Near the outset of 'Building, Dwelling, Thinking', Heidegger declares: 'To be a human being means to be on earth as a mortal. It means to dwell' (PLT, p. 147). There is a great deal of Heidegger's later philosophy packed into these two sentences. We might begin the work of unpacking by connecting what he is saying here to some of the central ideas of 'The Origin of the Work of Art'. Though Heidegger nowhere in these later essays invokes the notion of earth as something that struggles with world, which suggests that we cannot readily assimilate the earlier and later thoughts, nonetheless the appeal to earth again emphasizes the *grounded* character of human existence. Human existence is a materially real phenomenon, situated in particular locales with particular features to which human beings must in some way accommodate themselves. The appeal to earth also calls attention to the ways that human beings are *dependent upon*, and so *indebted* to, their surroundings for such basic things as food, water and shelter: 'Earth is the serving bearer, blossoming and fruiting, spreading out in rock and water, rising up into plant and animal' (PLT, p. 149). Heidegger's invocation of earth is his way of reminding us of our need for such basic forms of sustenance (that we need *reminding* is itself of special significance for Heidegger).

11A THE FOURFOLD

While in 'The Origin of the Work of Art' earth was paired with world, locked together in a kind of endless strife, Heidegger's appeal to earth in these later essays depicts it as intertwined in a considerably different manner. Earth is no longer paired with world, but instead bound up with *three* further notions, whose unity Heidegger labels the 'fourfold'. Two of those four interconnected notions are evident in our starting citation, since Heidegger there appeals to *earth* but also *mortals*: 'The mortals are the human beings. They are called mortals because they can die' (PLT, p. 150). Another echo from earlier in Heidegger's philosophy is evident here, as his appeal to mortality carries significant traces of his existential conception of death that played such a significant role in *Being and Time*. Here, as in *Being and Time*, human existence bears a special, even unique, relation to death. Saying that human beings 'can die' may not sound like a distinguishing characteristic, as animals, indeed all living things, only live for finite periods of time and so, as we commonly say, die. When speaking of plants and animals, however, 'die' only means that their lives come to an end, but Heidegger insists that 'only man dies', since 'to die means to be capable of death *as* death' (PLT, p. 150). The significance of the 'as' here is that only human beings are capable of living with a sense of their own finitude (though in many cases, that sense may be muted by some form of denial or obliviousness), of leading lives bounded and conditioned by stages of growth, health and sickness, maturation and decline. Other living creatures pass through these stages, but without any sense of them as discrete stages standing in relations to others. A sick or wounded animal simply lives out its sickness, inhabits its injuries, such that its impairments just are its ongoing condition with no sense of loss or longing for a different way to exist; an animal, we might say, is encompassed by its present condition, which is as much as to say that its present condition is not manifest to it *as* just one condition among a spectrum of possible ones.

That human beings confront their condition as instantiating members of a spectrum of possibilities indicates their special relation to *time*: that the stages of human existence – birth, growth, maturation, decline and eventual death – are manifest *as* stages evinces the *temporal* character of human existence, as not just spread out through time but as involving an awareness and possession of time. Heidegger alludes to the uniquely temporal character of human existence in his explication of the notion of mortals; in doing so, he thereby invokes the remaining two dimensions of the fourfold: 'Only man dies, and indeed continually, as long as he remains on earth, under the sky, before the divinities' (PLT, p. 150). *Sky* is Heidegger's name for the temporal cycles that pervade human life, indeed all life on earth:

> The sky is the vaulting path of the sun, the course of the changing moon, the wandering glitter of the stars, the year's seasons and their changes, the light and dusk of day, the gloom and glow of night, the clemency and inclemency of the weather, the drifting clouds and blue depth of the ether. (PLT, p. 149)

Human existence, as grounded on the earth, at the same time always involves some accommodation to these temporal cycles. Human life is pervaded by significant *times*, where the source of that significance is something beyond human convention. How one acknowledges and prepares for the coming of winter versus the onset of summer is conditioned by the nature of those seasons. Doing different things at different times makes a kind of sense beyond just what we feel like doing or decide to do, though Heidegger's fear is that this is becoming less and less the case (witness as an example indoor ski slopes in the middle of the desert).

Heidegger's appeal to *divinities* is more enigmatic than the other three dimensions of the fourfold. It is not at all clear to me how literally to take his appeal to 'the god' and 'gods', insofar as it might be understood as a resurrection of some kind of polytheism. What Heidegger says about the divinities leaves what he has in mind rather cryptic: 'The divinities are the beckoning messengers of the godhead. Out of the holy sway of the godhead, the god appears in his presence or withdraws into his concealment' (PLT, p. 150). We might try to understand what Heidegger is saying as follows: when we think about human existence, the three dimensions of the fourfold already discussed appear to mark out important, if not essential features, of it. The grounded character of human existence, its being caught up in various temporal cycles, phases and seasons, and its ultimate finitude: all of these do appear essential to what human life is all about. Something, however, is left out, in the sense that there is another 'direction' towards which human existence often points, a direction which is neither down (earth) nor up (sky), nor towards the indefinitely finite future (mortals). That further direction is, we might say, *beyond* all of these, a kind of *transcendent* direction or dimension. We might call this dimension a 'spiritual' one, while leaving how this is to be cashed out deliberately vague. The deliberate vagueness leaves room for various ideas, various ways of talking and acting, ranging from the idea that we find some things 'special' or 'meaningful' in ways that separate them from quotidian concerns to direct, explicit invocations of transcendent entities (angels, gods, demons) and events (miracles, curses and the like). Such distinctively meaningful things might be the birth of a child, the way a landscape looks in a particular light, the intimate bond one feels with loved ones (which can be experienced more vividly at certain times rather than others), the beauty of something found or created. Things can also be meaningful in much darker ways, as when one suffers a devastating loss, hits what feels like (and perhaps in retrospect turns out to be) a low point in one's life, or experiences a sudden, surprising reversal. These sorts of episodes and events naturally invoke the language of *blessing* and *curse*, the *sacred* and the *tragic*, the *holy* and the *abominable*, and this language is not readily assimilated to other categories (such as economic or market value, where everything 'has a price'). This language can be further articulated in more explicitly divine or theological directions, but it need not be (one can feel blessed without necessarily thinking of that blessing as coming from someone or somewhere in particular). With or without the extra theological 'spin', the pervasiveness and irreducibility of these ways of experiencing indicate a kind of transcendent dimension to human life.

Heidegger takes great care to emphasize the unity or 'simple oneness' of the fourfold, which means that these four dimensions are ultimately inseparable from one another: insofar as one starts with any one 'fold', one will inevitably be led to the others. For example, spelling out the earthy dimension of human existence quickly leads to what Heidegger calls sky: the ways human existence is grounded in the earth is inflected by temporal cycles, significant times and dates. Part of being grounded on earth is being subject to seasons, to maturation and decline, birth and death (notice how quickly we've ended up at the notion of mortality), and this subjection can variously show up as a blessing or a curse, an occasion for gratitude or despair, sometimes one and sometimes the other. What Heidegger calls *dwelling* is living in a way that incorporates and acknowledges the unity of the fourfold: to dwell is to occupy or inhabit the fourfold *as* a mortal, which means living in a way that is grounded in the earth, accommodated to the cycles of life and responsive to intimations of transcendence latent in daily living.

11B TECHNOLOGY AND THE FOURFOLD

According to Heidegger, human beings have a kind of duty to 'spare' or 'save' the fourfold, which again means living in ways that fully acknowledge these mutually implicating dimensions of life and experience. All too often, however, Heidegger thinks that we *fail* really to dwell, that our duties go unattended and forgotten. What this means is that human beings often live in ways that variously resist or deny the four dimensions Heidegger names in his articulation of human dwelling. While there are many sources for this resistance, its fullest manifestation is the technological understanding of being. Indeed, what Heidegger in 'The Question Concerning Technology' refers to as the 'supreme danger' of modern technology might at least in part be understood as the ways in which technology undermines the kind of dwelling he describes. What is it about technology that threatens dwelling? We might answer this question by reflecting on technology's impact with respect to each of the four dimensions of the fourfold:

1. Earth: As we have seen, technology, as enframing, transforms what there is into a vast system of resources. This transformation denies to things their particularity, treating what there is as flexible, interchangeable resources to serve various needs and purposes. Heidegger characterizes this transformation as placing an 'unreasonable demand' for energy on the earth itself, but it also threatens other earthy dimensions of human existence. For example, technology has a way of depriving *places* of their particularity by making anywhere and everywhere equally available and in various ways. Modes of transportation have become ever more efficient at moving people from one place to another, but I can also be elsewhere without leaving my room: I can turn on the television, get online, pick up a phone and so on, and thereby be transported beyond my immediate surroundings. Heidegger complains that this 'frantic abolition of all distances' brings no 'nearness', in the sense that we fail to attend to the particularity of what surrounds us. More radically, we might say that technology makes it increasingly the case that what surrounds us no longer really has any particularity: the kind of homogenization brought about by the ever-increasing scale of corporate dominance is evidence of this. Across the United States (and elsewhere), one encounters pretty much the same stuff: the same places to shop, to eat, to buy coffee or a book; the same movies and television to watch, the same kinds of internet hook-ups. The net effect of this sameness is that one is always nowhere in particular, because there is no longer any particular place to be.

2. Sky: In 'Building, Dwelling, Thinking', Heidegger characterizes those who dwell as not turning 'night into day nor day into a harassed unrest' (PLT, p. 150). Turning night into day means living in ways that fail to accommodate the temporal cycles that mark out our lives; it means living in a way where the difference between night and day is obliterated or effaced, but also the difference between summer and winter, warmer climates and cooler climes (witness the ubiquity of air-conditioning and refrigeration), drier and wetter regions (consider the presence of golf courses, even rice paddies, in what would otherwise be desert landscapes). A worry arises here though as to how one distinguishes between accommodation and effacement. For example, do I fail to dwell every time I turn on the light in my study after dark? If Heidegger's views had this

implication, that would make them vulnerable to easy dismissal. There are two ways one might go here. On the one hand, it could be said that turning on a light is a way of acknowledging and accommodating the darkness of night. Simply switching on my light to read in my study does not turn night into day, since my activity retains the character of being conducted at night rather than in the day (my study at night has an entirely different 'feel' to it than in the daytime). Turning night into day would be more like living constantly in an artificially lit environment, where it no longer mattered what time of day or night it was (and one could no longer really tell just by looking around). On the other hand, it could be argued that turning on a light hides a whole complex array of relations and activities that have far greater ramifications than we usually like to ponder. The use of my light requires electricity, which is supplied by wires connecting my house to a vast network that traces back to a coal-fired power plant miles from my house. That plant requires a constant supply of coal mined from the earth and delivered by hulking trucks that consume vast quantities of fuel derived from crude oil that is also extracted from the earth. Both the plant and the trucks, the mining and the drilling, damage the earth by destroying vast stretches of land- and seascape and throwing pollutants into the air, whose devastating effects are only now becoming fully understood. All of this is implicated in my casual flick of the switch: that I rarely pay heed to these implications when so flicking is testimony to my inattentive relation to my world. My activity is instead driven by the demand to read whenever and wherever I want, which is what the supply of electricity allows me to do.

3. Mortals: The flick of a light switch is emblematic of the ways technology promotes a stance of ease and flexibility that seeks to overcome the barriers traditionally imposed by natural temporal cycles (day and night, summer and winter, sickness and health). Technology thereby transforms human existence into a kind of ongoing demand for ease and flexibility (one-touch, one-click, all-in-one, just one push of a button convenience), for the ever more immediate satisfaction of whatever desires one happens to have. 'Availability on demand' is something of a watchword for modern consumption, which means that to be a consumer means to demand, regardless of time of year or time of day (provided, of course, that one is willing to pay). Though this looks like a kind of mastery, living in such a manner means being little more than a shifting cluster of

demands, which can itself be effectively ordered. Life itself thus becomes something to be optimized, effectively ordered and indefinitely extended, so that the course of one's life is no longer marked by indelible and irrevocable changes. (Of course, life still is so marked, but technology presents the erasure of such markers as a kind of ideal.)

4. Divinities: We have already seen that technology fosters the illusion that human beings are *masters* of the earth. Our ever improving ability to order resources effectively and efficiently expresses our dominion over the earth. This aura of dominion threatens to deprive life of any of the intimations of transcendence Heidegger associates with divinities. If *everything* is a resource, then everything is (merely) something to be ordered and exploited, to be optimized according to whatever standards are currently in place. In a world consisting only of resources, nothing has any kind of intrinsic sanctity because nothing has any intrinsic character whatsoever.

Heidegger argues that all of the different aspects of humans' failure to dwell is condensed into our relation to *things* (again, we can see how Heidegger's early concern with things in 'The Origin of the Work of Art' slowly evolves into a preoccupation). He writes:

> Staying with things, however, is not merely attached to this four-fold preserving as a fifth something. On the contrary: staying with things is the only way in which the fourfold stay within the four-fold is accomplished at any time in simple unity. (PLT, p. 151)

What Heidegger here calls 'staying with things' ultimately involves renewed attention to the nature and possibilities of *language*. We thus need to return to the invocation of Hölderlin's phrase, '. . . poetically man dwells . . .', in order to trace these connections.

11C LANGUAGE, POETRY AND THE (RE)COLLECTION OF THINGS

Commenting on the idea that science annihilates the thing, Heidegger remarks:

> The thingness of the thing remains concealed, forgotten. The nature of the thing never comes to light, that is, it never gets a hearing. This is the meaning of our talk about the annihilation of the thing. That annihilation is so weird because it carries before it

a twofold delusion: first, the notion that science is superior to all other experience in reaching the real in its reality, and second, the illusion that, notwithstanding the scientific investigations of reality, things could still be things, which would presuppose that they had once been in full possession of their thinghood. (PLT, p. 170)

Although this passage begins with an appeal to *forgetfulness* as our current relation to the thing, the 'twofold delusion' Heidegger goes on to explicate serves to complicate that idea. The first aspect of the delusion is unsurprising, as it reiterates Heidegger's hostility toward a hegemonic conception of the sciences as having a kind of exclusive claim to revealing how things (really) are; the second aspect, however, gives one pause, as it suggests that things have yet to come into 'possession of their thinghood'. Heidegger continues by noting that things 'have never yet been able to appear to thinking as things' (PLT, p. 171). These passages have the net effect of reorienting our understanding of Heidegger's mourning, since it now appears to have the form of a kind of pessimistic longing, a desire for something that might yet be but faces overwhelming difficulties in coming to pass. These passages also help to deflect the charge that Heidegger, in his longing for the thing, is simply indulging in nostalgia, despite his predilection for rustic and rugged examples. As he himself acknowledges toward the end of 'The Thing': 'Nor do things as things ever come about if we merely avoid objects and recollect former objects which perhaps were once on the way to becoming things and even to actually presencing as things' (PLT, p. 182). Indeed, if we take these passages seriously, it is not clear that there really are any examples of things, but at best approximations.

That examples of things are not ready to hand is, for Heidegger, bound up with the idea that we dwell unpoetically. What Heidegger calls our 'restless abolition of distances' (PLT, p. 166) near the outset of 'The Thing' is symptomatic of this failure. That our lives have become 'frantic' and 'restless', that we live in such a way that 'everything gets lumped into uniform distancelessness', suggests a kind of pervasive inattentiveness, a failure to attend to things in their particularity. Science transforms things into objects, and technology condemns us to objectlessness. Heidegger sees poetry, and the fundamentally poetic nature of language, as the antidote to this kind of frantic oblivion. 'The poetic', Heidegger claims, 'is the basic

capacity for human dwelling' (PLT, p. 228). Whereas science annihilates the thing, effacing it through a kind of quantitative homogenization of space and time, poetry calls to things in their
particularity, thereby establishing (or holding out the possibility of
establishing) a kind of proximity to things. The act of naming
'brings closer what it calls', and so 'brings the presence of what
was previously uncalled into nearness' (PLT, p. 198). The act of
naming thus 'invites things in, so that they may bear upon men as
things' (PLT, p. 199).

Poetry names, calls and so invites things in their particularity
through the particularity of poetic language. What I'm calling here
the particularity of poetic language is revealed in the ways in which
poetic language has its own kinds of regimentation, its own
demands for order and exactitude, but of a kind other than that
found in the sciences. That a poem employs *this* word, rather than a
near synonym, with *this* stress and in *this* relation to the words
around it: understanding these demands is essential to a proper
understanding of poetry, of its peculiar kind of necessity. To substi-
tute words and expressions wantonly, even for more or less synonymous words and expressions, is to fail to grasp the nature of the poem
and of the poetic use of language. Language, we might say, *matters*
in poetry, and so it is in poetry that something essential about language is revealed.

In saying that language matters in poetry, I do not want to suggest
that Heidegger wants to call our attention to further, and otherwise
neglected, features of language, e.g. its 'aesthetic qualities' over and
above, or apart from, language's 'cognitive' dimension, its meaning
proper. Rather, Heidegger's conception of the poetic, of the poetic
nature of language, is more radical, as it aims to reorient our entire
understanding of the nature of language, and in a way which resists
these sorts of distinctions between the cognitive and the aesthetic,
between content and form. The reorientation Heidegger seeks is suggested by his distinction between 'speaking language' and 'employing language'. As he puts it in *What Is Called Thinking?*:

To speak language is totally different from employing language.
Common speech merely employs language. This relation to language is just what constitutes its commonness. But because
thought, and in a different way poesy, do not employ terms but
speak words, therefore we are compelled, as soon as we set out

upon a way of thought, to give specific attention to what the word says. (WCT, p. 128)

'To give specific attention to what the word says' involves a recognition of the particularity of the word, such that what we might otherwise be tempted to separate out into its aesthetic and cognitive features are bound together. To recognize the inseparability of these features is to recognize the word *as* a word, rather than as a *term*. As Heidegger acknowledges, such recognition may not be easy to achieve:

> At first, words [*Worte*] may easily appear to be terms [*Wörter*]. Terms, in their turn, first appear spoken when they are given voice. Again, this is at first a sound. It is perceived by the senses. What is perceived by the senses is considered as immediately given. The word's signification attaches to its sound . . . Terms thus become either full of sense or more meaningful. The terms are like buckets or kegs out of which we can scoop sense. (WCT, pp. 128–9)

Poetry, as Heidegger understands it, directs our attention to the words themselves, rather than terms that act as mere containers ('buckets or kegs') of their meaning. As Heidegger puts it, words 'are not like buckets and kegs from which we scoop a content that is there' (WCT, p. 130). Instead, 'words are wellsprings that are found and dug up in the telling, wellsprings that must be found and dug up again and again, that easily cave in, but that at times also well up when least expected' (WCT, p. 130).

The particularity of words in poetic language is of a piece with the particularity of the thing. 'The word makes the thing into a thing – it "bethings" the thing' (OWL, p. 151). Coming to appreciate the particularity of poetic language is thus a step at least towards coming to appreciate the particularity of the things called forth by the poem: by attending to the words themselves, we thereby come to attend to the things themselves. To insist on the possibility of redescription of the thing without acknowledging the loss that redescription might exact (redescribing the jug, say, as a material object – an aggregation of matter – rather than as a vessel, indeed *this* vessel, for pouring) is to fail to acknowledge the particularity of the thing. Recall what Heidegger says in connection with the jug:

In the scientific view, the wine became a liquid, and liquidity in turn became one of the states of aggregation of matter, *possible everywhere*. We failed to give thought to what the jug holds and how it holds. (PLT, p. 171 – my emphasis)

The particularity of poetic language – poetry's insistence on the importance of particular words in particular places – resists the kind of homogenization characteristic of scientific and technological understanding.

Coming to know the poetic, coming to take the poetic seriously, is Heidegger's way of talking about the possibility of redeeming the loss of things in our lives: fostering a reverence for the forms of language is a contribution to the realization of that possibility. While Heidegger cautions that realizing this possibility cannot be effected by 'a mere shift of attitude', since that alone 'is powerless to bring about the advent of the thing as thing', a change of attitude toward poetry and poetic language might still constitute a first step. Moreover, that change can in part be a matter of our coming to be receptive to Heidegger's own words, to the particular descriptions that constitute his progress toward the nearness of things. Earlier, I cited a passage from 'The Thing', wherein Heidegger describes his own way of looking at things, at the jug in this instance, as 'semipoetic'. Not yet poetry, and yet on the way to poetry, this description suggests, or rather demands, something from the reader, namely a willingness on the reader's part to take Heidegger's descriptions seriously as they are. Some of Heidegger's remarks on the example of a bridge in 'Building, Dwelling, Thinking' are instructive on this point (see especially PLT, p. 153). In particular, Heidegger insists that we not read his language as in any way *symbolic*, as though it treats the bridge as a symbol. Such a way of construing his language would be to treat it as in some way secondary or derivative, a way of treating the bridge beyond what it really is. To encounter the bridge *as* a thing *is* to encounter and describe it as it really is, but this should not tempt us to underdescribe its thingly character: 'The bridge is a thing and *only that*. Only? As this thing it gathers the fourfold' (PLT, p. 153). Heidegger's rejection here of the notion of the symbolic as a way of understanding his depiction of the bridge is of a piece with his demand that we come to take poetic language seriously, as getting at or getting to what things really are. Heidegger's talk of 'gathering', his invocation of the 'fourfold' as essential to characterizing the particularity of the thing adequately is apt to be dismissed as merely symbolic, as something superadded to how things really are. On the contrary, to be receptive to Heidegger, and so to be on the way to being receptive to poetic language more generally, one must come to recognize those 'semipoetic' descriptions not as symbols, projections, or fanciful imaginings, but rather as picking out genuine features of reality, ways that our lives might be shaped, ways in which our lives and the world we inhabit might genuinely matter.

11D THE STATUS OF HEIDEGGER'S LATER PHILOSOPHY

Since perplexity is what Heidegger enjoins us to cultivate and attend to, it is perhaps fitting to end this book with something of a puzzle concerning his later philosophy. Actually, I want to gesture towards a cluster of puzzles, all of which arise in relation to Heidegger's guiding idea in his later philosophy. That guiding idea is the history of being: what Heidegger calls 'the truth of beings' in 'The Origin of the Work of Art' is something that changes over time in accordance with the opening and closing of different historical worlds. The notion that being has a history marks a significant departure from the outlook and aspirations of *Being and Time*, which sought to reveal the essential, more or less transhistorical, structures of Da-sein. *Being and Time*, we might say, sought to explicate Da-sein *as such*, whereas the later philosophy is far more suspicious of that idea (this way of drawing the contrast is, however, too simple, as we'll see shortly).

One puzzling feature of Heidegger's conception of the history of being concerns the relation between 'the truth of beings' and what we might call 'the whole truth'. As we have seen at several points, Heidegger seems to want to say that it is only from within some particular historical world, some particular opening or clearing, that things are manifest in some way at all, but at the same time, he seems to suggest that not all openings are equally revelatory. That is, he seems to allow room for the idea that some openings onto what there is may be in various ways distorting. This is especially evident in 'The Question Concerning Technology', at the point where he is spelling out the 'danger' associated with the very idea of revealing in accordance with any historically articulated 'essence'. After observing the corrosive effect of causal thinking on how God is revealed, he observes more generally:

In a similar way the unconcealment in accordance with which nature presents itself as a calculable complex of effects of forces can indeed permit correct determinations; but precisely through these successes the danger can remain that in the midst of all that is correct the true will withdraw. (QCT, p. 26)

Notice that this passage, by distinguishing between 'the true' and the correctness of the determinations made from a scientific perspective, leaves room for a kind of truth of how things are beyond how they are manifest from within some particular understanding of being. This in turn suggests that whatever Heidegger means by 'the truth of beings', it cannot be exhaustive of the notion of how things are.

That there is a kind of mismatch – indeed, Heidegger suggests at some point that such a mismatch is inevitable – between the truth of beings and what I'm calling here the whole truth is in accord with Heidegger's contention that every historical world, as an opening onto what is, is always in some ways partial or aspectual. The very idea of changing historical worlds would seem to require some kind of partiality or perspectival character, as otherwise it would not be clear how any such change could come about. Every world, while in some ways revelatory (and essential for the occurrence of any revealing at all), at the same time obscures some things or some ways things are. What this means is there is always some truth about how things are that is unavailable from within any particular historical world. But if the availability of truths about how things are is keyed to occupying a historical world, how can Heidegger (or anyone else, for that matter), as a denizen of a particular historical world, have any kind of access to those otherwise unavailable truths? If the opening of a historical world really is the condition of the possibility of revealing – if the opening of a historical world just is what revealing is – then the possibility of getting a glimpse of something beyond any such opening should not even make sense, let alone be actualized in Heidegger's philosophy. This is, by the way, an instance of a problem that arises with trying to make sense of relativism more generally: the more seriously one takes the claims of relativism, the more difficult it becomes to understand how those claims are possible. If truth is relative to a culture, and everyone occupies some culture or other, then there is no room for the transcultural apprehension of the relativity of truth. Insofar as this apprehension *is* possible, then truth is not really relative to a culture but transcendent with respect to any, indeed, all of them.

That Heidegger treats the revealing that happens with the opening of particular historical worlds as partial, aspectual or perspectival shows that he is no simple relativist. The ways things are outstrips any particular historical understanding of being, which is part of what motivates changes in that understanding. Moreover, Heidegger has the resources to address the worry just raised about availability, i.e. the problem of how any occupant of a particular historical world can have a sense of something beyond or outside that world. We must keep in mind his conception of the *essence* of human beings as involving the possibility of a kind of 'free relation' towards the core understanding of whatever world they inhabit. (Here we can see that Heidegger has perhaps not strayed as far from the aspirations of *Being and Time* as we might want to think: that human beings have an *essence*, even in his later philosophy, suggests that he is still in some ways interested in working out what Da-sein is 'as such'.) To *think*, for Heidegger, means to occupy that free space and in that way make manifest what is otherwise unavailable to those who only inhabit the current historical world.

While Heidegger can assuage the worry about the availability of what ought to be unavailable truths or insights, his way of doing so gives rise to two further puzzles about his later philosophy, neither of which admits of a ready solution. The first puzzle concerns the question of assessment: How are we to adjudicate, or assess the merits of, the claims Heidegger makes with respect to what is manifest from the perspective of this 'free space'? What standards are we to use to evaluate different claims made by those who take themselves to occupy such a perspective? Standards of evaluation would seem to be part and parcel of the different historical openings onto what there is, in that one way of understanding what a change in world comes to is the decline and rise of different such standards. For example, those who inhabited the world opened up by the Greek temple had very different standards for evaluating actions (as heroic or cowardly, for example) than those who living in the world of the Medieval cathedral (where actions might be sinful or saintly). Clearly, those standards are not going to be of use for something beyond, or outside of, what those openings afford access to, but what other standards are there? Heidegger would seem to face a dilemma here. On the one hand, if he proposes standards, that would seem to undermine the master idea of the later philosophy. That is, if there are standards for evaluation that transcend the standards deployed by various historical worlds, then the opening of a historical world is not equivalent to revealing. On the other hand, if there are no standards, then it is hard to know what to make of *anything* that is presented as being offered from this 'free' perspective. How does one know when that perspective has even been attained, either by someone else or even in one's own case? To his credit, Heidegger is very much alive to this worry, and to the extent that he addresses it, he appears to opt for the latter horn of the dilemma. Consider, for example, what he writes in the Epilogue to 'The Thing' concerning what he calls responding to 'an appeal of being': 'But precisely here the response may hear wrongly. In this thinking, the chance of going astray is greatest. This thinking can never show credentials such as mathematical knowledge can' (PLT, p. 184). That such thinking can never 'show credentials' would appear to be tantamount to saying that there are no standards by which to evaluate that thinking. The difficulty with simply embracing the second horn of the dilemma, however, runs deeper than just telling the difference between 'going astray' and getting things right: the problem is one of what any such difference is supposed to be. For his part, Heidegger wants to insist that his kind of thinking, while lacking credentials, 'is just as little a matter of aribitrariness; rather, it is rooted in the essential destiny of being'. The puzzle, though, is how this is anything more than insistence here: what makes some thoughts genuinely 'rooted', while others are not?

Even if Heidegger has the resources to solve this puzzle (and I very much want to leave open the question of whether he does or not), there remains a further puzzle. This last puzzle concerns the relation between what appear to be two competing ideals in Heidegger's later philosophy: the ideal of *thinking* and the ideal of *dwelling*. As we have seen, Heidegger appeals to dwelling as something essential to being human: insofar as we fail to dwell, we thereby fail to realize our essence. Dwelling is something human beings should strive for, and the clear implication is that we (and the earth) would be better off were we to achieve that condition. But dwelling, as a kind of wholehearted belonging with respect to the fourfold, would appear to be at odds with what Heidegger calls thinking. Thinking, as the occupation of the 'free space' wherein 'questioning is the piety of thought', seems to require a kind of detachment rather than belonging. The thinker stands apart from how things are manifest so as to maintain a 'free relation' to whatever historical understanding of being prevails, but that free relation is incompatible with the prevailing of *any* historical understanding, not just the current one. Thus, when Heidegger, at the close of 'Building, Dwelling, Thinking', discusses 'the plight of dwelling' and 'man's homelessness', it is not clear what the net effect would be of bringing 'dwelling to the fullness of its nature' (PLT, p. 161). Though he says that this fullness can be brought about when we 'think for the sake of dwelling', the peculiarity of this claim is that its achievement would mark thinking's end. Thus, we are left to wonder whether what Heidegger calls 'homelessness' is ultimately a problem to be overcome or a state to be cultivated. Would the end of homelessness also be the end of philosophy?

SUGGESTIONS FOR FURTHER READING

WORKS BY HEIDEGGER:

As indicated by the small number of abbreviations used for citing Heidegger's work, I have made explicit use of only a small handful of his writings. There are, of course, many others (a complete edition of Heidegger's work – the *Gesamtausgabe* – comprises some 102 volumes), some of which have been lurking in the background of my presentation. The following are some works available in English that I think are especially good for continuing exploration of many of the ideas discussed in this book.

Early Heidegger:

In general, I have found Heidegger's lectures from the years surrounding the writing and publication of *Being and Time* very illuminating for understanding that book; they are also in many ways far more accessible due to Heidegger's less formal lecture style. Here are some additional titles beyond the two (*The History of the Concept of Time* and *The Basic Problems of Phenomenology*) cited in the text:

Fundamental Concepts of Metaphysics: World, Finitude, Solitude, trans. W. McNeill and N. Walker, Bloomington: Indiana University Press, 1995.

Introduction to Phenomenological Research, trans. D. Dahlstrom, Bloomington: Indiana University Press, 2005.

Metaphysical Foundations of Logic, trans. M. Heim, Bloomington: Indiana University Press, 1984.

Ontology – The Hermeneutics of Facticity, trans. J. van Buren, Bloomington: Indiana University Press, 1999.

Towards the Definition of Philosophy, trans. T. Sadler, London: Athlone Press, 2001.

Later Heidegger:

Nietzsche: Volumes One and Two, trans. D. F. Krell, New York: HarperCollins, 1991.

Nietzsche: Volumes Three and Four, ed. D. F. Krell, New York: HarperCollins, 1991.

Pathmarks, trans. W. McNeill, Cambridge: Cambridge University Press, 1998.

WORKS ABOUT HEIDEGGER:

The secondary literature on Heidegger is vast, and the newcomer is apt to be bewildered by the variety. To assist in finding a way in, I have assembled a number of works that are readily available and likely to be useful to readers who are still learning their way around Heidegger's philosophy. Many of these volumes have their own bibliographies, which will direct you to further, more specialized reading.

Blattner, W. *Heidegger's* Being and Time: *A Reader's Guide*, London: Continuum, 2007.

Dreyfus, H., *Being-in-the-world: A Commentary on Heidegger's Being and Time, Division I*, Cambridge: The MIT Press, 1991.

Dreyfus, H. and Hall, H., eds, *Heidegger: A Critical Reader*, Oxford: Blackwell, 1992.

Dreyfus, H. and Wrathall, M., eds, *A Companion to Heidegger*, Oxford: Blackwell, 2004.

Dreyfus, H. and Wrathall, M., eds, *Heidegger Reexamined* (four volumes), London: Routledge, 2002.

Guignon, C., ed., *Cambridge Companion to Heidegger*, Cambridge: Cambridge University Press (second edn), 2006.

Kisiel, T. and van Buren, J., *Reading Heidegger from the Start: Essays in His Earliest Thought*, Albany: State University of New York Press, 1994.

Mulhall, S., *Routledge Philosophy Guidebook to Heidegger and Being and Time*, London: Routledge, 1996.

Polt, R., *Heidegger: An Introduction*, London: UCL Press, 1999.

Wrathall, M., *How to Read Heidegger*, New York: W. W. Norton, 2005.

Wrathall, M. and Malpas, J., eds, *Heidegger, Authenticity, and Modernity: Essays in Honor of Hubert L. Dreyfus, Volume 1*, Cambridge: The MIT Press, 2000.

Wrathall, M. and Malpas, J., eds, *Heidegger, Coping, and Cognitive Science: Essays in Honor of Hubert L. Dreyfus, Volume 2*, Cambridge: The MIT Press, 2000.

INDEX